Phillip R Greaves 2ND

Ψ

SOCIETY, REASON, SEXUALITY

THE DOMINIONS OF MAN*

COPYRIGHT © 2012

All Rights Reserved

---

2   **Society, Reason, Sexuality**   2

2   **Knowledge is Power**   2

Other Books by
Phillip R. Greaves, 2ND@

Society, Reason, Sexuality • Our Fountains of Pleasure, Truth, and Order • 4 Your Consideration • The Power and Virtue of Lust • The Grand Delusion • A Government of Service to All • Water and Oil: Religion and Sex • Water and Oil: Sex and Government • Water and Oil: Government and Religion

@ Titles generally available off and on line, in digital and analog formats.

4   **Society, Reason, Sexuality**   4

4   **Knowledge is Power**   4

5   Society, Reason, Sexuality   5

To Allan: Please forgive me and come back.

6   **Society, Reason, Sexuality**   6

6   **Knowledge is Power**   6

Section Directory

SOCIETY
9
REASON
133
SEXUALITY
245

8   Society, Reason, Sexuality   8

8   Knowledge is Power   8

Society

A FREE COUNTRY FOR A FREE PEOPLE

12   **Society, Reason, Sexuality**   12

It is not the purpose of the law to provide a livelihood for attorneys, judges, administrators, or legislators. These are just side effects of the law. Its real purpose is to provide a framework for the peaceful interaction and coexistence of men and women within a common social structure. This purpose is most efficiently achieved when all citizens are fully informed of the content and effect of the law.

Contents

ONE EQUALS INFINITY

THE STATEMENT ONE EQUALS INFINITY is not intended as a mathematical formula, nor as a description of the universe, though it applies (the infinity of the one universe). No, this statement is meant as a political description stating the proper relationship between any individual and the masses in a free society.

The actual meaning of one equals infinity is this: the rights of men are not accumulative, men do not acquire any greater degree of their fundamental rights by joining together into groups or mobs. A collection of men has no more authority or primary rights than those held by an individual alone.

***

This is not the end of democracy, however. Democracy will continue to operate as it always has: as a decider of issues, and the ranking of men/women. We will still have to vote for the issues and vote for the workers, the President, Congress, etc. But changing the

Constitution should be even harder than it now is. I suggest a four-fifths vote to add an amendment and the placing of certain provisions beyond even the vote of the people, least it become too easy to lose those hard-earned rights.

What will change, however, is that there shall no longer exist an eminent domain authority. Instead, there shall be a fine, against the government, of seven times the value of anything commandeered, to be paid to the individual from whom anything was unlawfully taken.

No individual will ever again be forced to surrender their lawfully held possessions, to any authority or group, except as a penalty for the unlawful violation of another's fundamental rights. Under such a system, taxation shall be phased-out and ended. Within a system of true equality, government shall be funded through voluntary means such as use and service fees, donations, and games of chance.

Instead of property taxes, there shall be a general, municipal, use and service fee that will be applied to all the uses property taxes were once applied to (except for the fire department, which should be funded by all homeowner's insurance companies operating within a given city or town), the non payment of which may result in a lien against the property of any noncompliant resident or property holder.

Such a lien may be levied against any

and all properties owned by an individual, or business entity, for the non-payment of the GMUASF, but no confiscation of property may occur until the amount owed equals at least seventy-five percent of the full value of said properties.

The rationale for the GMUASF is pretty straightforward and obvious. Certain aspects of living in a community, which benefit all a city's citizens and residents, are simply better and more efficient when planned, maintained and administered by the local, municipal authority.

Some examples include roads and highways, parks, public schools, law enforcement, jails and prisons. There are several additional constraints on the

GMUASF with regard to who will be required to pay it and how it will be calculated.

First, no one under the age of twenty-one shall be compelled to pay this charge, so that the youngest wage earners may enjoy their full income and accumulate some savings prior to assuming the full responsibilities of adulthood.

Second, no one earning less than twenty thousand dollars per year shall be called upon to pay this fee, regardless of their age, as their income should be exempt from any mandatory expense being added to their cost of living.

Third, the GMUASF shall be no greater than one third of the estimated annual city budget divided equally among all city residents over the age of twenty-one with an income greater than twenty thousand dollars per year. Toward this end, there shall be a yearly census taken to determine who shall be charged this expense in the following year and how much they will be required to pay.

Fourth, those that are required to pay this use and service fee will have four options for doing so, annually, semi-annually, quarterly, or monthly.

Fifth, anyone paying the GMUASF who fails to earn the requisite twenty thousand plus dollars, in a given year, may demand a refund of all moneys they have paid in for that year in the beginning of the following year.

Sixth, in any year that the revenue from

the GMUASF exceeds one third of the estimated annual city budget, said overage shall be equally divided and returned to all those that paid into it. If there is anything remaining above this division, it must be placed in a savings account to earn interest, which the government can take as revenue and keep.

The principle, however, must be returned to the next drawing. The obligation to return such excesses to those who contributed to them may not be mitigated or suspended by either the legislature or the general populace. Any person that wishes his share left for the use of the legislature may donate it back after receiving it.

It is a long-standing position of the legal

establishment that ignorance of the law is no excuse. This position was originally based on the belief that the law should be a matter of common sense, easily discernable with just a little reflection. So laws such as those against murder, rape, theft, trespassing, etc. required little in the way of mental effort or education to conceive and understand. Matters are not so simple today.

The law has become an enormous and complex subject requiring a great deal of education, discipline, and effort to comprehend and apply. Under such circumstances, ignorance of the law can only continue to be dismissed if the law is made readily and equally available to all. This is not the situation that exists today.

It is not the purpose of the law to provide a livelihood for attorneys, judges, administrators, or legislators. These are just side effects of the law. Its real purpose is to provide a framework for the peaceful interaction and coexistence of men and women within a common social structure. This purpose is most efficiently achieved when all citizens are fully informed of the content and effect of the law.

Two ancient examples illustrate this position: Hammurabi, the greatest ruler of ancient Babylonia (1792-1750 B.C.E.), is best known for his code of laws, which he posted throughout his kingdom, so none would be ignorant of his decrees; and the Hebrew nation's requirement that male children memorize the Torah, which includes the law of Moses, prior to their thirteenth birthday and bar mitzvah (coming of age ceremony).

Such solutions as memorization or posting our laws in the town square, for all to see, are no longer practical. The complete laws of our land are too numerous to be memorized by any person, and they are too frequently changed, and added to, for a permanent display to be efficient. However, this does not mean the populace must go largely uninformed regarding the law.

No, there is an effective way to provide every citizen with an up-to-date copy of the laws that govern the common person, and a way to make specialty laws available to those they apply to. A general law book can, and should, be provided from each level of government to every resident and citizen, on an annual basis[1].

The telephone companies do this and our governments can too. It's the right thing for any government to do. No person should have to go to some high-priced lawyer, or his seat of government, just to become informed of the law. The legal system should bring the laws to every individual.

It is a national tragedy that the United States, the nation that considers itself the freest in the world, now imprisons more of its

---

[1]   Alternately, and more economically, these rules and regulations could be uploaded to the internet where they would be readily available for anyone to print out at their own expense.

citizens than any other country on Earth. This shame is caused by two aspects of the legal system, with regard to our laws and our treatment of criminals.

Our prison sentences are often of excessive duration and over fifty percent of the people serving them are there because of the war on drugs. These two factors have propelled our system of prisons and corrections into a rapid growth endeavor and, in some cases, a private enterprise.

The longer people are kept in a prison, the faster the space runs out, and the more people put behind bars, the quicker the need to build more correctional facilities. Don't misunderstand, murderers should be executed within ten years of their conviction.

However, many other prisoners are given excessive sentences.

Many people imprisoned for drug offenses are sentenced to thirty, forty, fifty or more years. This is ridiculous. Such people shouldn't be in custody at all. Any individual should have the sovereign right to control their own body, and that includes what they may put in their body, and what substances they may choose for recreation.

Other criminals are also given extreme sentences that reflect a public desire for revenge[2], rather then a need to safeguard the

---

[2]   Sex offenders fall into this category and, depending on whom you ask, are either the most, or the least, likely to re-offend. Where they are most likely to be repeat offenders, it is because there are no effective

community or reform the transgressor. Such overly lengthy prison terms serve no legitimate purpose, inhibit reform, promote dependency, and prolong the public's burden and expense.

A workable solution would be to limit prison terms to a maximum of ten years per

---

programs to help them reform, redirect, and reorient their sex drives, or to augment these efforts with masturbation. Prison administrators and personnel are generally hostile toward inmate masturbation, which results in an abnormally high level of aggression within most correctional facilities.

incarceration. If a criminal is sentenced to a term of less than a decade, and afterwards is found guilty of additional crimes, their term of imprisonment may be raised to as much as the ten year limit. Under no circumstances, however, may any prisoner be sentenced to more than the ten-year limit, per internment in any correctional facility.

Such a solution would greatly reduce the public's burden and expense, promote reform and independence following a prisoner's release back into the general populace. This limitation would only apply to terms of imprisonment.

Financial obligations, however, may be imposed without limitation, per each crime an individual commits. Such monetary compensation may be collected either by confiscating a criminal's property or by garnisheeing their income, after their release from prison.

Only a garnishment of fifteen percent may be made against any person's income, and that must be evenly divided among all claimants until each is paid in full, regardless of how long this may take, or until the offender shall die.

This correctional strategy is to be applied to every criminal and every crime, except for murderers and murder, regardless of the emotional magnitude of the crime. So, thieves, conmen, counterfeiters, robbers, spouse-beaters, rapists, kidnappers and child-molesters[3] will all be treated according to this plan.

Many people, reacting emotionally, will be angered that rapists, kidnappers and child-molesters[4] would receive no more than a

---

[3]   The most despised offender is the pedophile or "child-molester," as society tries to protect juveniles from the "corruption of sex." This extreme hatred of "child-molesting-pedophiles" is misdirected, due to the media's misrepresentations and its failure to distinguish between the pedosexual-pedophile (child-lover) and the pedocidal psychopath (child-killer). So most people confuse one with the other, believing that pedophiles are child-rapists and murderers. This, of course, is untrue. From the way people react, one would think being sexually molested, or even raped, is the worst thing that could possibly happen to a child. Well, I can think of a few other things that are easily worse, like losing the use of an eye, hand, or leg, being paralyzed, suffering brain damage, being disfigured, etc. I would much rather be sexually "abused" then to have any of these other things inflected on me.

[4]   In 2008CE, the Supreme Court of the United States issued a ruling that child-rapists may not be

ten-year-sentence, but they should consider the issue logically.

Instead of moaning that the sentences should be longer, or death, they should consider the effect that death and life sentences have on the victims. Would they rather have survivors of these crimes, or corpses? The problem goes all the way back to the Bible. If you're going to be stoned to death for using the "Lord's" name in vain why shouldn't you also disrespect your parents,

---

sentenced to the death penalty unless their actions resulted in the death of their victim(s), as this would be cruel and unusual punishment.

commit fornication, adultery, rape, kidnapping, murder, etc.

After all, you're going to die anyway, and you can only be killed once. A death sentence is a death sentence, a life sentence is a death sentence too, because you're going to die in prison ether way.

The eighth amendment to the United States Constitution states, in part, "Excessive bail shall not be required, nor excessive fines imposed,..." Yet the reality of our present judicial system is that excessive bail is often required and excessive fines are routinely imposed, but this is treated as a mere difference of opinion between the justice system and the accused.

With regard to the justice system,

excessive bail and fines are those in excess of the magnitude of the crime and are compared to the bails and fines set for a particular crime throughout the country.

The legal system views both bails and fines as a means to fund the judiciary and prevent the flight of the accused. In certain cases, such as murder, bail is intentionally set so high that it is extremely unlikely that the defendant will be able to post it. At other times, bail is flat-out denied.

Our eighth amendment, however, was not written and added to the United States Constitution in order to empower the justice system, but to protect the rights of the accused. With this intent, the issue of what is excessive revolves around the resources of the defendant.

This means that bails and fines[5] are excessive whenever they exceed what the accused can afford, above his established financial commitments: such as food, housing, utilities, medications, and existing loans. The rational approach would be to require proof of a defendant's resources, prior to setting any bail or fine, and then to set such accordingly and fairly.

Our right not to testify against ourselves is acknowledged in the fifth Amendment to

---

[5]   The court would do well to note that these abusive penalties punish/harm more than just those convicted. Such excessive demands for money also hurt the defendant's family, taking the food from its children's mouths, as well as its landlord, utility providers, insurance agencies, and each of the convict's loan holders. In short, such fines harm our general economy.

the USC[6]. Here also the court has twisted the meaning of the law, so that it not only protects us from any demand that we incriminate ourselves, but also prohibits us from testifying in our favor.

This is a travesty of justice. To be withheld from baring witness in our favor is to be compelled to bare witness against ourselves. To say nothing in one's favor is to legitimize everything said against one.

Surely, the most amazing amendment to

---

[6]   The fifth Amendment does not say that you can only avoid incrimination by remaining silent. Silence can incriminate one as easily as a confession. Necessarily then, this prerogative must include the right of a defendant to lie on the stand without threat of penalty. A defendant, therefore, should never swear any oath to tell the truth, as this actually negates one's right to avoid self-incrimination.

the USC[7] is clearly the fourteenth, which grants, to every citizen of the United States, the same rights and immunities under Federal law and equal protection of the law within every state. Its only real failing is that it only guarantees the right to vote to males over the age of twenty-one. That is why the nineteenth amendment was necessary to guarantee women the right to vote.

The fourteenth, however, did not deny the right to vote to either women or those under the age of twenty-one, but rather left this up to the states, as does the twenty-sixth with regard to those under the age of eighteen.

---

[7]   United States Constitution

Furthermore, if taken to its logical extreme, the fourteenth amendment also eliminates the age and residency restrictions, in the main body of the national constitution, regarding who could legally run for office, including the Presidency of the United States. Now it is not only native-born Americans that can run for the highest office, but naturalized citizens as well.

One cannot have equal protection of the laws without having the same laws applied to everyone. Therefore, if, in any state, a woman has the legal right to marry a consenting man, so too must a man have the legal right to marry a man, and the same goes for a man marrying a woman and a woman marrying a woman.

Calling gay marriage something other than marriage is just that old "separate but equal" scam that was tried on blacks not too many years ago. This doesn't mean, however, that any church or faith should be required to perform or accept gay marriages, but any that wish to certainly may. The only person who should be drafted to perform gay marriages is the Justice of the Peace. If he can not handle that part of the job, then he should resign.

Also, if a heterosexual couple has the right to adopt, in any state, so too must a homosexual couple have that right. Private adoption agencies and orphanages must be allowed to discriminate, however, if we are to be true to the one equals infinity position that the rights of the one are equal to the rights of the many.

When convicted criminals enter our jails and prisons and become wards of the state, they retain many of their civil rights, but not their civil liberties. They retain the right to legal counsel, the right to communicate with the outside world, the right to receive visitors, and the right to religious worship and practice.

Among the things they lose, however, are their freedom of motion, their independence, privacy, freedom of choice, some of their dignity, and most of all their ability to participate in the political life of our nation[8]. Convicts are not allowed to run for

---

[8]   Although I favor allowing prisoners the right to

office or even vote. The rationale behind these political restrictions is to prevent the prison population from having any direct effect on the laws and conditions related to their incarceration.

Such a goal is misguided, at best. In any democracy, the prison population is simply too small to make a significant impact in the electorate with respect to any particular issue or candidate. Furthermore, the prison population is no more likely to vote as a

---

vote in public elections, I fully support the ban against their running for public office while they are in jail or prison, for obvious reasons.

unified block than is the general populace.

On the positive side, allowing prisoners to vote would encourage them to see themselves as still part of the greater community (which they are), and to interact with it in a peaceful and rational way. It may even help them to reintegrate into society when their release comes due.

In ancient times, thirteen-year-olds were considered to be men and permitted to sit at the counsel of men and other tribal meetings. In the United States of America, the age of consent varies from thirteen to nineteen, but only those over eighteen are allowed voting rights throughout. California has voted on two occasions (so far) to give voting rights to sixteen-year-olds. The issue failed on both attempts, but the fact that the measure made it to the ballot (twice) shows that the subject actually had quite a lot of support.

Many people think that the twenty-sixth amendment to the United States' Constitution establishes the minimum voting age for the whole country, this isn't correct. While the twenty-sixth amendment does require that eighteen-year-olds be given the vote everywhere, it doesn't prohibit the states from allowing even younger citizens the right to vote. My own position on this matter is two fold. First, anyone, of any age, who serves in our military, should automatically have the right to vote in our elections.

Second, there should be a citizenship

test where anyone who passes will be given full citizenship rights, including the right to vote and engage, as an adult, in consensual sexual activity, along with drug and alcohol consumption. This test should be open to everyone from five to twenty. No one who hasn't achieved adulthood, by growth or by test, should ever be tried as an adult in court.

The government should be allowed to compete with the private sector in any endeavor it may choose, provided that any such enterprises be started, funded, operated and maintained by voluntary means, to include free-market sales and purchase, contest, lotteries, donations, etc.

Originally, the purpose of Social Security was to provide an allowance for the retired, the aged, and single mothers. There is no reason why this program cannot be continued, but it must become a voluntary program funded by voluntary means. Later, Social Security was expanded to include health care through Medicare and Medicaid. These programs can also be continued under a voluntary format.

A great deal of money can be saved for these programs if the government would stop paying above market value for medical equipment. Our government's medical programs often pay double or more for the same items that cost half as much or less on the open market. A box of latex gloves, for example, cost around seven dollars in the private sector, but Medicare pays over fourteen dollars for the same item.

There is a very old, but underhanded and dishonest business practice that must be ended. I am speaking of the use of fine print on contracts and advertisements. The only reason that fine print is employed is to hide important information where the vision-impaired and careless will not see it.

While it's true that prices may go up, temporarily, the benefit to consumers will be enormous, as they will be more thoroughly informed with regard to their choices in the marketplace.

I think all businesses, licensed within Pueblo, should be prohibited from using any print smaller than a twelve-point font on all contracts, advertisements and promotions after a given date.

There should be a hefty fine for any breach of this law. The only exception to this rule should be for advertisements and contracts that are printed in only one font size.

TAX-FREE AMERICA

Our forefathers made one mistake. What they should have fought for was representation without taxation.

--Fletcher Knebel

And you're working for no one but me.

(The Beatles, "Taxman")

EVERYONE HAS HEARD THE OLD SAYING, "...nothing is certain but death and taxes.[9]" This statement, while certainly true of death, is mistaken regarding taxes. There are many ways to avoid taxes. If you want to avoid sales tax on certain items (such as food, labor or clothing), there are States you can move to where these items are not taxed. If you want to avoid state income tax, there are also states which do not tax income. Our federal government even allows certain tax-breaks to the chosen few who qualify.

---

[9] This well known saying comes to us from the last line of a quote of Benjamin Franklin.

But, if you want to avoid taxes altogether you have only two choices. One choice is to do all your business with unlicensed businesses and individuals which claim no income or property. Such businesses and persons neither collect nor surrender taxes. Your other choice for avoiding taxes is to support and promote voluntarily funded government[10] This means fighting for the right to keep and control your own money.

The black market has two major advantages over voluntarily funded government: It is already here, and nearly everyone uses it. Every time anyone sells

---

[10] The possibility of voluntarily funded government is examined in the fifteenth chapter of "The Virtue Of Selfishness," by the late philosophical giant Ayn Rand.

something to a friend or a stranger, and fails to declare the income, collect or surrender taxes, they are part of the black market. The black market, however, has many very real dangers. Among these dangers are real criminals hiding from the law and trading illegal goods and services. Murderers, rapists, thieves, and conmen hide and do business on the black market alongside the otherwise honest tax-dodger.

Furthermore, governments believe they have a right to a part of everyone's income and property without regard for anyone's personal consent. For these reasons governments have declared the black market illegal. If you are caught doing business on the black market, the government may legally take all of your property, and/or imprison you. If you resist arrest, you may be shot and killed. If you want to avoid the dangers of the black market, and still escape taxation, your best choice is to support and promote voluntarily funded government.

Under voluntarily funded government you decide when, if and how much of your money goes for the support of government. As long as you respect the property rights of others, the government may not claim any part of your property without your uncoerced agreement.

There are two main problems with voluntarily funded government, however: It is not currently available, and it has never been tried. Because it has never been tried, many of us are at a loss as to how voluntarily funded government might work. After all, who would just give money to the government?

Every day millions of us make promises and commitments to others and depend on the promises and agreements others make with us. These promises and commitments are contracts -- verbal and written -- relating to everything from marriage vows to the exchange of goods and services. The court system exists, in part, to make sure these promises are kept. Currently, the expense of our court system is paid for by taxes and fines. Under contract insurance, fines would continue to pay for part of court system expenses. Taxes, however, would be replaced by optional contract insurance.

With contract insurance, our government would only protect those contracts which had been insured by the payment of a premium in the amount of a legally fixed percentage of the sums involved in the contract. This insurance would be voluntary, there would be no punishment for those who failed to buy it -- they would be free to make verbal agreements or sign uninsured contracts, if they chose.

Such contracts, however, would not be legally enforceable. If an uninsured contract were broken, the injured party would have to accept their losses -- their only recourse would be to spread a bad word and refuse to do future business with the contract breaker(s).

At this point, it must be understood that contract insurance need not require our government to make good on any of the contracts it insures, except for its own. Our government need only insure the right to a fair trail to determine the guilt and responsibility of the contract breaker(s). When awards are granted to the victim(s), our government may either award the victim(s) and require reimbursement from the guilty, or require direct payment by the guilty to the victim(s).

With regard to contracts of a more personal nature, such as marriage vows, an escape clause could be included or assumed (if omitted or excluded) to limit the responsibility of any party choosing to void the contract.

In most cases, however, voluntary contract insurance would work like a sales tax. Many of us would routinely insure the quality of products such as food, clothing, etc. by choosing to pay the contract insurance fee. In addition, optional contract insurance could even be used to insure foreign contracts, goods and services. This, in turn, would add foreign moneys to the support of our court system -- reducing its cost to us.

The vast majority of all contracts are fulfilled without any recourse to the courts. Revenue resulting from contract insurance fees would, therefore, greatly surpass the needs of the court system. This excess revenue could be applied to the funding of all other governmental services. The largest share of this revenue would come from the most productive and wealthiest individuals and businesses. This is as it should be because these have the greatest values to protect and, therefore, the most to lose from broken contracts.

It should now be obvious that this form of voluntarily funding government could easily fund all necessary government services at a rate of under ten percent per contract. The revenue generated could be split among city, county, state and federal agencies to cover every level of governmental service.

Another method for voluntarily funding the government would be a national lottery.

Such a lottery already exists in many foreign countries and several of our own States also hold lotteries. These lotteries bring in enormous sums of money -- both monthly and annually.

Such lotteries have never been used to eliminate taxes, but there is no real reason why they couldn't or shouldn't. A national lottery could easily have several levels of winners ranging from a few dollars to, perhaps, a billion.

With optional contract insurance, a national lottery could be open to foreign players, adding foreign moneys to the support of our government. Government's share of lottery proceeds could be used to support governmental agencies and services at all levels -- that is, local, county, state, and federal.

Just as optional contract insurance would draw most of its revenue from the rich and upper-middle-class, so a national lottery would draw most of its revenue from the poor and lower-middle-class without causing any undue hardship among the lottery's participants. Such a lottery could be split among city, county, state and federal agencies to cover every level of governmental service.

Ideally, such a split would give the largest revenue shares to local and federal agencies because they have the smaller revenue base to draw from. The local agencies, however, should receive the largest share of revenue (collected in their area) as the most immediate areas of service.

Although such a lottery could support our government on its own, if the lottery were used in addition to optional contract insurance it would guarantee the success of voluntarily funded government.

So far, I have mentioned two methods of voluntarily funding the government (optional contract insurance and a national lottery). I have explained how each would work and some of their benefits. Each of these methods is based on providing some benefit beyond funding government in general.

In the case of optional contract insurance, the direct benefit is the ability to sue contract breakers -- individuals, groups, organizations. The direct benefit of a national lottery is the chance to win a large jackpot or smaller prize. In both of these cases, funding our government by voluntary means is a secondary benefit. There is, however, a more direct, if more questionable, way to voluntarily fund our government. This would involve direct donations to our government for the sole purpose of funding its services and agencies.

To understand how funding our government by direct donations could work, consider the methods used to fund charities. Examples are many. Churches, for instance, pass around collection plates, hold fundraisers, and even ask their supporters for special donations for many causes. Many churches are enormously successful at getting what they ask for. Other charities employ television, radio, mailings and door-to-door solicitors in their efforts to raise money for their many causes.

Many of these charities are extremely well funded. In all cases, however, the funding of these charities comes just for the asking. It should not be too difficult to foresee many of us routinely donating money to our government for the support of the military, the police force or the court system[11]. It is even easier to envision us

---

[11]   The only things worse than a tax supported police force, court system and/or governing body, are any which are financially dependent on criminal fines and penalties, as these represent a conflict of interest. When crime is high, these generate large sums of money for such agencies, which they quickly become dependent on.

frequently sending donations to our government to support its many charities.

The fact that governmental funding

Then, when crime abates, they suffer from a lack of revenue. Calls for higher taxes quickly follow to make-up for these shortfalls. Although fines and penalties may act to deter crime, when they are enforced, the only way to remove the conflict of interest, they create, is to disperse all these funds to non-governmental, non-religious, randomly selected, charities. As an alternative to taxes, penalties, and fines, governmental telethons might prove successful. Radiothons might also be employed for such purposes.

through donation is not connected to providing any direct benefit to the donors (apart from funding our government), however, makes it the least likely method for funding our governments without taxes. Optional contract insurance and a national lottery are more likely to succeed in this purpose.

Nevertheless, direct donations to our government are an excellent way to fund its many charities and social programs. Donations are, in fact, the most moral method of funding our governments' charitable activities.

It should now be clear that it is possible to replace tax funded government with voluntarily funded government. This fact, however, raises three very important questions: (1)Why should voluntarily funded government be preferred over taxes? (2)If voluntarily funded government is so much better, why are we still being taxed? (3) How can the change from taxes to voluntarily funded government be brought about?

The reasons that voluntarily funded government should be preferred over taxation are both moral and practical. The wage earner, the businessman, the land owner all have an absolute right to the whole of their property -- having gained it through voluntary trade and being free persons. No one, not even a government, should be allowed to gain any part of their property except through the same method of voluntary trade.

Whatever is taken from its owner(s) without their   consent is stolen. Taxes, because they are taken in this manner, are stolen property. A government has no more right to steal for an alleged public good than a robber has to steal for a favorite charity. When a government claims a right to steal, by what right can it punish others for doing the same?

The government that taxes commits robbery.   Furthermore,   an   individual's property is its life. A government that claims a share of any individual's property, apart from their consent, enslaves them. A person who is taxed is not free. They are owned by the government taxing them.

Practical reasons for preferring voluntarily funded government to taxes relate to cost savings and putting the control of our government back into the hands of each and every one of us. The cost saving benefit of voluntarily funding government is fairly straight-forward. Eliminating taxes means eliminating tax returns and the cost and paperwork associated with them. This is no small benefit for the government or the rest of us.

Under our current tax system, the cost of tax refunds and the filing of tax returns consumes a large share of tax revenues and results in enormous governmental, corporate and personal headaches. What voluntarily funded government receives in revenue, through this method of funding, would be fully available for its use in providing its services. The size, power and function of the IRS would be greatly changed and reduced.

The greatest practical benefit, however, would be the much improved ability to hold the government in check. Every individual, within a government's area of service, would be empowered to withhold their share of government's funding any time they discovered their government overstepping its bounds, infringing the rights of its clients, misusing the funding it receives or providing inadequate service relative to its level of funding.

They might also, rightfully and occasionally, apply their resources to a more urgently considered need or goal. The right of an individual to freely allocate government's funding should be recognized as an essential right, on the same order as freely electing one's representatives in government.

All this raises the question of why we are still being taxed. After all, if voluntarily funded government is workable, achievable and clearly better, why are we still bearing the burden of taxes? The answers to this question are multiple and relate to tradition, the nature of government and corruption.

Taxes are the traditional means for funding government, going all the way back to the tribute demanded by tribal chiefs and kings as landlords and supreme rulers. Before the American Revolution, the government of every nation was headed by a king and/or queen who ruled over their people. The purpose of government was to command, control, direct, guide and manage its people.

People were the wards, servants, and often the slaves of the kings. Private property was nonexistent. A king owned both the land and his people. Whatever possessions his people held, they held by the king's permission. The American Revolution radically changed the very nature of government.

America's founding fathers viewed government as our servant -- the exact opposite of the traditional view. They saw the individuals among us as sovereign, with fundamental and irrevocable rights.

America's founding fathers held that the purpose of government was to protect and defend the rights of individuals (within a government's area of service) from any violation of their rights by other individuals, groups or governments. For this purpose, America's Founders created a representative government, ". . .of the people, by the people, and for the people."

So radical and so great were the achievements of our founders in creating a fundamentally new kind of government that they should not be greatly blamed for failing to establish a voluntarily funded one -- especially considering that the constitution they wrote provides the means to correct this mistake. Nevertheless, taxes are a flaw corrupting the great American experiment of a free country for a free people.

The worst mistake (the one which keeps the others in place) America's founding fathers made was calling the thing they created government. The word government belongs to the enemies of freedom.

Government comes from the Greek word meaning to steer or guide. To steer or guide is to control, direct and manage. (You steer a horse, you steer a car, you do not steer a man). This is the old definition of government.

It is very difficult to change the definition of a word. It is much easier, more effective and more efficient to create a new word, or to use a short description. If

America's founding fathers had called their creation a national security service, most of their other mistakes would already have been corrected. A national security service lacks the parental air of a government.

Without the parental air of authority, American freedom would have already reached its full and proper growth. Americans (and many others) would now enjoy the maximum level of personal freedom allowed by reason, fairness and justice. Serious crime would be the rarest of things.

Government's parental air, however, can only be maintained through taxation. Without compulsory funding (taxes), our government would either have collapsed or surrendered the last of its parental authority long ago.

The combination of a parental attitude and taxation, however, have led to an enormous failure for the experiment in freedom. Instead of a national security service dedicated to the growth and security of rational, individual rights; we have a parental government directing all of us for the alleged good of the national family. So, here is the old government commanding each of us as to what we may or may not do, and how much of our money we may keep for ourselves.

Here we have the spectacle of elected representatives creating excuses (agencies, programs, wars, social objectives) to reach deeper and deeper into the pockets of individuals -- who may not refuse -- in order to impose order that is neither desired or needed, seeking to gain prestige that is not deserved.

A disdain for government's parental attitude, however, should not be viewed as a rejection of proper law and order. Proper law and order are essential to the security of any society. Without such order, individual freedom would be impossible.

The necessary limits of freedom and guidelines for proper law and order are described by two simple principles: (1)No individual, group or agency may violate the person or property of a non-consenting other. (2)Doing so requires the violator to forfeit values of comparable worth.

Anything beyond these two principles is oppression and tyranny. The purpose of law and order then is to protect each of us against any violation of our person or property, and to insure reparations (where appropriate) from any violator thereof.

Some of the primary reasons we are still burdened with taxes are that few of us are aware of the possibility of voluntarily funded government and our elected representatives are unwilling to surrender their ability to reach into our pockets at their convenience. This brings us to the question of how the change from taxes to voluntarily funded government can be achieved.

America's change from taxes to voluntarily funding government cannot be achieved immediately. Before taxes can be eliminated, voluntarily funded government must first be established. Optional contract insurance, a national lottery and donations must be put into operation before taxation can be abandoned.

The security of our nation requires that government funding be continuous throughout the change from taxation to voluntarily funded government. The first step, therefore, is to educate everyone concerning the possibility of voluntarily funding government and to encourage them to notify their representatives of the demand for its creation and establishment.

NO MORE REGESTRATION

It has been over thirty years since then-President-Jimmy Carter pardoned the Vietnam area draft-dodgers, suspended military conscription and established the selective service system as an emergency, call-to-arms. Thus were America's all-volunteer-forces born, and served us well they have and do. And yet, our politicians refuse to put their complete trust in a military that isn't driven by the whip.

From its top brass to its greenest private, almost no one, among today's troops, wants a return to the days of compulsory service. Nearly everyone acknowledges that a volunteer makes a better, more loyal and effective soldier than most any man made to service his country by force.

Furthermore, a drafted force is an affront to the nation that demands one. A draft implies that the citizenry is so apathetic toward, disgusted with, or oppressed by their politicians, they'd rather be overrun by an invading force than defend their homes. This has never been a problem within the United States.

Although the United States has often employed the use of conscription, it has never actually needed to. Her citizens have always stood ready to defend their homeland and the principles upon which their nation has been founded. Although ignored and denied, these very principles, as expressed in our Constitution's thirteenth amendment, demand that the use of a military draft, and any mandated registration for such, be permanently abandoned and abolished.

Composed and ratified, following America's civil war, the thirteenth amendment reads, "**Neither slavery nor involuntary servitude, except as a punishment for crime whereof the party shall have been duly convicted, shall exist within the United States, or any place subject to their jurisdiction.**" To the best of my knowledge, it is not a crime to be male, eighteen or under the age of twenty-six. Nor have I ever heard of anyone being convicted of these "offenses."

For those who would exempt mandatory service from the province of the thirteenth amendment, by referring to the general welfare clause of the Constitution's preamble, I will simply point out that amendments always override everything that precedes them in the event of a contradiction. Were it otherwise, do-gooders could claim that prohibition is still in effect because the amendment that created it came before the one that ended it.

Not being one to call for civil disobedience, I encourage every- one touched, or moved by this issue, to write their governor, and con- gressmen, urging them to do the right thing and have the instrument of the draft, and any registration related to such a device, officially and permanently, prohibited under any and all circumstances.

***

It has been long over due, and I join my brothers and sisters in their celebration. I only hope our jubilation is not premature. Allowing soldiers to openly claim their homosexuality, is one thing, actually permitting gay sexual behavior, in on post housing, or in town, is something else, altogether.

If it has not already been addressed and revised, the military code of justice needs to be modified to allow the sexual conduct that defines our kind and our culture. This code regulates every aspect of a soldier's life (on and off post) and prescribes penalties for any breach thereof. It even seeks to govern a soldier's sexual conduct.

When I served, heterosexuals were only allowed reproductive style intercourse, and everything that could be described as gay sex: sodomy, fellatio (sorry ladies no fun for you either, *and I can not find the spelling*) were prohibited and punishable. If this hasn't been changed, then it needs to be. Allowing sexual openness, while requiring celibacy is not acceptable.

Besides, many straight boys and girls like sodomy and oral sex too. Don't you? Yeah, you know it.

NOTHING BUT MARRIAGE

Don't let anyone fool you. Marriage is not a contract between those getting married and the State. Our governments should do nothing more than to perform these ceremonies, or to act as witness to these events. It should not have any voice in marriage apart from this. Government should not presume to select or approve the spouses to be.

Marriage is an agreement, between those marrying, to love, respect, and honor each other for the rest of their lives. It should not be viewed as a license to have children, nor a demand that one should. The traditional vows do not even mention having children or raising them.

It is not a right, purpose, or power of government to define or regulate marriage. Nor should any church be allowed to define or regulate marriage beyond their own membership. Certainly, not by force of law. There is no church that can rightfully claim a copyright on the institution of wedlock.

Society itself is not qualified to define the meaning or character of matrimony for any of the individuals of which it is formed. The rights of the many are never greater than the rights of the one. Marriage should be defined exclusively by those being married and those intending to marry.

The fourteenth amendment to our

national constitution (USC[12]), clearly states, in its first clause, "All persons born or naturalized in the United States, and subject to the jurisdiction thereof, are citizens of the United States and of the state wherein they reside. No state shall make or enforce any law which shall abridge the privileges or immunities of citizens of the United States: nor shall any state deprive any person of life, liberty, or property, without due process of law; nor deny to any person within its jurisdiction the equal protection of the laws."

Except for requiring that the States grant twenty-one-year-old males the right to vote (in its second clause), the fourteenth

---

[12] United States' Constitution

amendment makes no distinction among citizens on the basis of class, gender, race, age, sexuality, wealth or political/religious affiliation.

No special rights for the rich or the poor, black or white, male or female, young or old, gay or straight. Everything a citizen is, one is. For each citizens is a citizen, and every citizenship is the same. No legal distinction among the Hindu, atheist, Jew, Christian, or agnostic.

I would think that our rights and immunities probably begin with those presented in the first ten amendments to our Federal Constitution, and every citizen is entitled to them. But these are the rights of individuals, institutions do not have rights.

Now the States are required to provide equal protection under the law, but equal protection can not be achieved unless the same law is applied to everyone. All States recognize a woman's right to marry a man and a man's right to marry a woman, but all citizens must have the same rights. Until men share with women the right to marry men, and until women share with men the right to marry women, all parties consenting, the genders will never achieve true political equality.

Recently, The Connecticut Supreme Court ruled that separate wasn't equal. Anything less than marriage violated equal protection laws. Homosexuals do not want any marriage equivalency status, passed by any State, chiefly because the rights granted by such an instrument wouldn't follow them from State to State as legally binding, nor would it have any effect on an individual's status under federal law. In sort, nothing but marriage will do. Besides, a word is not copyrightable. Its meaning is always open to change.

Also recently, California had an election to determine the status of gay marriage, as to whether or not the Californian government would continue to recognize such unions. A hoard of Mormons descended on California and stayed long enough to vote on the measure themselves. Rarely have I been so disgusted by these meddlesome, religious pricks and their continuous interference in matters that really do not concern them.

Gay marriage isn't going to impose any obligations on them at all. Nothing will require any church to accept or perform gay marriages or weddings. The only person that will be drafted in this affair will be the Justice of the Peace. Only this office will be required to perform such services. The religious interference on this issue has only one real goal and that is to impose religious, "moral" values on the rest of us through political force, and this, above all else, should be illegal.

Once an amendment, defining the conditions, rights and liberties of citizenship has been passed (such as the fourteenth amendment to the USC), no common law, or amendment to any lesser constitution, should ever be entertained by any legislator, or presented to the public for a vote, regarding any aspect of the amendment in question, as it will automatically supersede and cancel any such effort.

No, an amendment can only rightfully be modified or replaced by a new amendment at the same governmental level (or higher). It is up to the judiciary to determine if a particular situation or circumstance falls under the authority of a given amendment and not an issue for the electorate to decide.

Sooner or later, I hope it's sooner, the issue of gay marriage will reach the Supreme Court of the United States. I am confident the highest court will rule in favor of gay marriage and the right of homosexuals to define marriage for themselves.

SINGLE GENDER FAMILES

The actual rearing of children is beyond the scope of this paper. What I would like to present, however, are the many ways by which homosexuals can become parents and the advantages and disadvantages of each.

Many people wrongly assume that because homosexuals aren't sexually inclined toward the opposite sex, they have no interest in raising children. This is a very mistaken notion. Other people feel strongly that homosexuals set a bad example, and therefore, shouldn't be allowed to raise kids.

This prejudice is also in error. Once a child has come into such a family, gay parent(s) are fully able to do all the same things heterosexuals would do for the care and nurture of their children. But having children, in the first place, is a little more complicated for them.

Perhaps the easiest way for a homosexual to become a parent is to adopt the children of a lover who was previously part of a heterosexual union. It may be difficult, however, to find a potential mate with this qualification.

You would be a stepparent and might not receive much respect from your new brood. After all, they already have a mom and dad, why would they want a stepparent at all? Before you can assume the position of well loved and respected stepfather, you must make friends with the children.

Another way for homosexuals to become parents is for them to engage in heterosexual intercourse strictly for the purpose of procreation. Arrangements regarding the custody of the pending child may be decided on the basis of the child's gender: a little girl would become the child of its lesbian mother and her spouse, while a boy would become the child of the gay couple that includes his sire.

There are other variations regarding this reproductive strategy. Instead of the sperm coming from one member of a gay couple, a different donor may be employed. Egg donors are also available. There may be fees to pay donor(s), surrogate(s) and doctor(s).

If it's important for the child to receive its genes from at least one member of a given couple, and heterosexual intercourse is considered undesirable, artificial insemination may be used instead. In any event, the health, condition and appearance of the pending child should be considered carefully.

Finally, a homosexual couple might opt for adoption. Adoption allows one to select the characteristics considered most important, and the aesthetics values too, as they are already expressed in a living child. The medical files are generally available on children awaiting families.

Unfortunately, many adoption agencies are unwilling to consider single-gender families.   Fortunately,   there   are   many agencies and some of them will consider gays as potential parents.

UNCONSTITUTIONAL

I can not speak with respect to the entire municipal ordinance under which we, the people of Pueblo, live but if the nuisance laws are any indication, things are pretty bad all over. At several points, within the nuisance ordinances, these laws are in direct violation of our National Constitution as the supreme law of the land.

Our nuisance laws contain a provision allowing a code enforcer to identify and declare a nuisance, even if it is not enumerated within the text of the law. This is arbitrary, unfair and violates due process.

It's arbitrary because it depends entirely

upon the whim of the inspecting officer, which makes it unfair, as the violation cannot be identified and avoided beforehand. This violates due process because such an offence rest upon the decree of an individual. Any other law would be debated in counsel (or in public) before being voted into law. It's so much more then this, though. The enforcer also has the power to abate said infractions, without giving the property owner any notice at all. The owner will soon get the bill.

Now the code enforcer becomes, not only jury, judge and executioner, but legislator, as well. When was the code enforcer ever elected to its position? This is a violation of our Nationally guaranteed right to due process. Additionally, these ordinance violate a defendant's right to a jury trial as well as the court appointed attorney guaranteed to the poor.

There are no Constitutional grounds for denying anyone a trail by jury. Most certainly not because the Court has set a time limit on declaring one's prerogative. Nor because some municipal authority wants a twenty-five dollar jury fee. Both of these conditions are Constitutionally invalid.

Additionally, one's entitlement to Court appointed counsel does not depend on whether or not one faces a possible jail sentence. The only Constitutional restrictions on this provision are that one must be unable to afford an attorney on one's own and that the amount in dispute (one's fine, for example) be greater than twenty dollars.

Our Federal Constitution forbids excessive fines and bales. And, as the eighth amendment was added to the United States Constitution to protect the rights of the defendant, these involuntary expenses are excessive whenever they exceed the liquid assets of the accused minus their other obligations.

The court would do well to note that these abusive penalties punish/harm more than just the convicted. Such excessive demands for money also hurt the defendant's family, taking the food from its children's mouths, as well as its landlord, utility providers, insurance agencies, and each of the convict's loan holders. In short, such fines add to our current recession. Whatever is unconstitutional is also illegal.

The true purpose of the law is to provide a framework for the peaceful interaction and coexistence of men and women within a common social structure. It is a fact that this goal is most efficiently reached when every citizen/resident is fully informed of the content and effect of the law.

Pueblo has done a very poor job of getting these laws into hands of we common folk. It actually seems that the public authorities of this city do not really want the text of our laws in the hands of the people. Sure, they have a website which contains these laws, but it can be difficult to find them even after one finds the website.

Once you find them, you will also notice how user unfriendly they are. To save you some unnecessary trouble, here is the full address to all our many laws and ordinance http://www.pueblo.us/cgi-bin/gt/tpl_page.h tml,template=1%26content=368%26nav1=1% 26 I strongly suggest that everyone printout (even if you have to go to the library to do so) a copy of these municipal laws, 'cause that's where all the loopholes are.

By all men call holy, such Constitutional abuses and due process violation may make our city a sitting duck for some eager lawyer to launch a very large class-action suit. This could cripple our economy. I would really hate to see that happen, we all suffer too much all ready.

I also advise that advertising the internet site of our laws be carried-out in the following manner: first, get all the television stations, operating locally, and the cable and dish companies, to advertise the complete address at lest three times a week, during peak hours. Second, include the newspaper for at least one prominent add spot per week.

The local radio stations should also share in this responsibility and announce the address at least three times a day, during prime broadcast hours. I am certain you can get this done with the television and radio folks, as these must have their licenses renewed from time to time, from the good people down at City Hall.

LOCAL MAGISTRATE ERRS

The stunningly-attractive, silver-haired-magistrate, who boasts of authoring the woefully inadequate, meagerly-informative-pamphlets at our new, municipal, court house, is so in love with his own efforts that he is willfully blind to their shortcomings.

Indeed, he fails to give proper consideration to his presumed, public audience, the first rule of writing and communication in general. Surely, these pamphlets aren't intended for the consumption of lawyers or paralegals who are well informed of the language, content and context of the law.

It is not the purpose of the law to provide a livelihood for attorneys, judges, administrators, or legislators. These are just side effects of the law. Its real purpose is to provide a framework for the peaceful interaction and coexistence of men and women within a common social structure. This purpose is most efficiently achieved when all citizens are fully informed of the content and effect of the law.

While the term arraignment is defined, in the court's pamphlets, as an individual's first appearance, a large segment of the population has only the vaguest idea of what this term means, which they generally got from such television shows as "Law and Order."

Furthermore, most people are going to be ignorant of the terms and conditions, identified in these pamphlets, until their first court appearance, by which time it is too late (under Pueblo's municipal law) to request/demand a jury trail, or court appointed attorney. The Court uses these facts to railroad defendants and fleece the public.

It should be required that the accused be given these pamphlets with their first notice of any violation. I may be a bit naïve, but I know of no provision in our Federal Constitution (the supreme law of the land) allowing anyone to deny a defendant's demand for a jury trial for any reason, much less a failure to make such a demand in a "timely manner," before hand. A jury trail is a right of every defendant and a matter of their prerogative alone.

Additionally, the pamphlets state that a defendant's first appearance will be before the court, this is incorrect. There is a difference between making a plea in the courthouse and making it before the Court. One should rightfully expect to make one's plea before, at least, an officer of the court, which a mere clerk is not.

What is worse, however, is that these clerks pretend to be ignorant of the contents of Mr. Alexander's pamphlets and pur-posefully resist any request that might result in additional expense (such as a jury trail) for the court.

Reason

THE GRAND DELUSION

OR, WHAT HAS "GOD" TO DO WITH IT?

Curiously, the supporters of the "Intelligent Design Theory" reject the idea that the universe is self-existent, because of its compound nature, but accept blind chance as the explanation for their "God's" existence. It seems to me that the more basic something is, the more likely it is to be a primary existent.

Contents

ABOUT "GOD"

THE REAL TRUTH ABOUT "GOD" is that "It" does not exist. No supreme being commands the universe or watches over our lives. An Omnipotent, omniscient, all seeing ever-just-entity does not exist to make things right in the end. No ever-present-father exists to reward the good and punish the wicked. "God" is just a beautiful and frightening lie passed from one generation to the next, in the vain search for ultimate truth and meaning.

Compelling evidence for these claims can be found in the explanations which follow. Peruse them for your own enlightenment and the awakening of others. Also discover the only way in which "God" actually does exist, to the disappointment of every true believer.

SLAYING THE DRAGON / DEBUNKING THE MYTH

OBVIOUSLY, the most unassailable argument against the existence of "God" relates to

"Its"[13] many contradictory characteristics. At one and the same time, this "supreme being" is supposed to be eternal and omniscient. However, if we consider the nature of the eternal (the ever-existent) and knowledge, we discover none can possess both properties[14].

Knowledge must be stored, arranged and expressed through many interconnected, conceptual elements, and any entity possessing this quality must conform to and support

---

[13]   The pronoun "It," when capitalized and appearing in quotes refers back to "God" because the words "He," "Him" and "His" indicate sexual distinctions and suggest a female counterpart which is soundly rejected by all monotheists.

[14]   Others have argued different contradictory attributes relating to "God," but I am the first to expose the disconnect between an eternal existence and any capacity for knowledge.

these parameters: such as a computer's many bits and busses, or a brain's many cells and connections.

This requirement is contrary to the nature of an eternal existent, which would have to be indestructible and unchangeable. But to be so, such an existent would have to be indivisible, a simple element made of one part only. Such a being would have no capacity for information or knowledge. So, "God" would either be subject to decay and, therefore, not eternal, or "It" would be dumber than a rock[15]. Because of this, no

---

[15]   The reason knowledge excludes its manifestation through an eternal existent, or agent is because knowledge requires a particulate medium through which to express and manifest itself, as every datum of infor-

mation requires both independence and connectivity, linking each datum to the rest. Dynamic information / knowledge structures all have one serious problem. They are compound existents, which all religions agree -- and science upholds, to be temporary and subject to decomposition, dissolution, decay, and destruction. An eternal object, or entity, would only be able to avoid these threats as an indivisible, super-solid, without internal divisions or particulates, but this excludes the eternal from the realms of knowledge. The difference between an immortal and an eternal may be instructive. An eternal being would exist always, without beginning or end, theoretically. But one must also be indestructible, or its existence would be conditional and temporary. An immortal, however, would have a beginning but, under normal conditions (for an immortal), no end. It would not be indivisible or indestructible, however. An immortal's existence would be conditional and indefinite. Unlike an eternal-fundamental, an immortal could be killed at any time, with sufficient force.

being can ever qualify as "God."

Yes, I am relying on the physical restrictions we must submit to, but it's not just us. Every being must obey them, as such is the nature of all existents. Furthermore, they are not only material limitations, but conceptual, mental and spiritual (these all mean roughly the same thing) conditions which must apply to all sentient beings.

No matter whom the knower or plain of existence, *the concept of a cat is not the concept of a dog, nor is the concept of a dog that of a bird. It is because of the differences that the knowledge of these things cannot be combined into a single datum expressing their distinct natures.*[16]

For me, the word metaphysical refers to the nature of things, whatever they may be. However, the word originated as a philosophical attempt to explain such things as thoughts, emotions, concepts, dreams, magnetism, hypnosis, the wind, light and an imaginary intelligence behind the universe.

Logic and reason are the golden twins of philosophy which have led us to the most complete, provable, understandable and testable explanations of these various items, along with the realization that "God" is, and always was, a myth.

---

[16]   All italics, boldface, underlines, and color usage are employed for emphasis. Parenthesis are used for reference and expansion.

It is a blatant contradiction to even imagine a being without physical form. Even energy has physical form. In the past, people believed matter and energy were different and separate things, but it is now known they are the same. Their oneness can be identified by the word mattergy (a word I invented); energy is merely matter in motion.

A formless being is a non-existent being because such an entity would occupy neither space or time. This would exclude it entirely from the realm(s) of existence, except within the imaginations of conceptual intellects like ours. It is mankind which has created the delusion of a "universal intelligence."

***

As for how "God" could exist in the least

material way, this would be as "It" already does, as a floating abstraction in the minds of men. "God" can only exist as a disconnected idea in people's heads. And this is "Its" ultimate position of power, as the irrational hosts to "God's" essence are constantly adjusting themselves to what they believe their "Deity" wants and expects. In this manner, this ideological "God" can reshape the world nature has birthed.

While it is correct to say there is no "supreme being," as the religious describe "It," every concept, valid or not, has its form in the minds of those who hold it. So a "God" of sorts exists in the mind of each believer, and if a believer performs an act of kindness, or builds a church, because they believe their

"God" desires it, and then it is their idea of an "ultimate authority" which inspired this behavior.

Of course this sort of "Divinity" is entirely dependent upon the human imagination and, therefore, does not conform to any external, independent or concrete reality[17]. "It" is a product of consciousness and is, therefore, inferior to the conceptual mind. The Religions all got it wrong. It was only after man invented "God" that "It" re-shaped humanity -- for in the image of man, "God" was made.

---

[17]   By and far, most of man's "spiritual" beliefs and experiences are the product of ancient man's struggle to understand such mental phenomena as thinking, imagination, dreams and hallucinations.

***

There is an argument for the existence of "God," which has become popular in recent years. It's called, "The Argument for Intelligent Design," and asserts that the universe, but most especially our world, is too complex and interconnected to have occurred by random chance. As I will explain, this fancy sounding argument is just as hallow as all the other "proofs" for the existence of "God."

An even better name for this argument would be "The Argument from Complexity," because that is its fundamental issue. However, complexity is both the essence of this theory and its undoing.

Just as man is more complex than anything he has created, so "God" would be more complex than anything "It" might cause to be. "It" would have to be so, because of the knowledge needed to make each and every existent.

Therefore, if the universe requires a maker, _because_ _of_ _its_ _complexity,_ so too would that creator need a maker of its own," and so forth. And again, by being complex, such a "God" would be subject to constant change and decay.

It is not chance, anyway, which shapes the universe and everything in it, nor the intelligence of any "supreme being," but simple causation. Causation states that every effect requires a cause, but not that every existent does.

Curiously, the supporters of the "Intelligent Design Theory" reject the idea that the universe is self-existent, because of its compound nature, but accept blind chance as the explanation for their "God's" existence. It seems to me that the more basic something is, the more likely it is to be a primary existent[18].

JUST A FEW MISTAKES

"But acquired infallibility is not a natural necessity; on the contrary, it is a ray of the

---

[18]   One difference between science and religion is that science tends to build everything from the bottom up, from the most simple to the most complex, while religion insist on building everything from the top down. Just imagine starting a house by building the roof two stories above the ground without supports of any kind

bounty of infallibility which shines from the Sun of Reality upon hearts, and grants a share and portion of itself to souls. Although these souls have not essential infallibility, still they are under the protection of God -- that is to say, God preserves them from error. ...If God did not protect them from error, their error would cause believing souls to fall into error, and thus the foundation of the Religion of God would be overturned, which would not be fitting nor worthy of God (SAQ[19] pg.172, 'Abdu'l-Baha)."

The above words are those of 'Abdu'l-Baha (1844-1921), one time leader of the Baha'i Faith and the authorized interpreter of his father's (Baha'u'llah's) writings. Although he doesn't say so with regards to himself in the above passage, it is universally accepted,

---

[19]   "Some Answered Questions," by 'Abdu'l-Baha, 1908.

within the faith, that he was among those to whom he referred as possessing the acquired infallibility mentioned above.

As such he is revered as beyond error. The passages we will examine hereafter will show this is not so. 'Abdu'l-Baha was just a man, as subject to error as any other human being.

It is not, however, the purpose of this essay to diminish or undermine 'Abdu'l-Baha's station within his faith or to single out the Baha'i Faith as a false system of belief. No, the Baha'i Faith and the writings of 'Abdu'l-Baha have been selected because of their consistent attempt to appeal to the rational mind though seemingly reasonable examination and explanation.

Most religions, and their texts, assume the existence of "God" and proceed from there without ever trying to prove this assumption. The Baha'i Faith, however, and 'Abdu'l-Baha's writings are different. In the book, "Some Answered Questions" 'Abdu'l-Baha attempts to prove "God's" existence in a rational manner. It is here where we will look next.

***

"One of the proofs and demonstrations of the existence of God is the fact that man did not create himself: nay, his creator and designer is another than himself (SAQ pg. 5, 'Abdu'l-Baha)."

In its original sense, the word create means to bring something forth into existence. No man or woman ever created their self because no one can exist prior to their origin. So, even "God" could not originate "Itself." But every woman and every man was created by their father and mother through the act of sexual reproduction. I see no room or need for "God" in this process.

However, if anyone insists man be brought forth from the elemental, such as the Bible describes, **"And the LORD God (Yahweh) formed man of the dust of the ground, and breathed into his nostrils the breath of life; and man became a living soul** (Genesis 2:7)," they need look no further than evolutionary theory for the solution.

Only the first self-replicating molecules were without president, everything after them was mutation, survival, adaptation and reproduction. In any event, no designer was necessary. Theologians have a very poor understanding of evolutionary mechanics. Their ignorance is expressed in faulty assumptions like the one that follows:

"Then surely the first man had neither father nor mother, for the existence of man is phenomenal (SAQ pg. 88, 'Abdu'l-Baha)."

Actually, according to evolutionary dynamics, the first man/men did have (a) father(s) and mother(s), but they were at least one mutation away from being fully human. Their fully human offspring would have been (a) mutant(s) with respect to their parentage, but would not have been so different from their kind as to make reproduction impossible.

***

'Abdu'l-Baha's next attempt at proving the existence of "God" begins: "<u>The</u> <u>contingent</u> <u>world</u> <u>is</u> <u>the</u> <u>source</u> <u>of</u> <u>imperfections</u>: God is the origin of perfections. The imperfections of the contingent world are themselves a proof of the perfections of God (SAQ pg. 5, 'Abdu'l-Baha)."

Now this is a rather odd sounding proof, for it seems a perfect being -- such as "God" is alleged to be -- would produce a perfect creation. For how could imperfection be the fruit of perfection? The very assertion is a contradiction the Judeo-Christian bible firmly rejects in its account of creation. According to the Bible, after each act of creation, "God" looks upon what "It" has created and sees it is good. The first chapter of this "holy" writ even ends with "God" overlooking all "It" had made and seeing it is all good.

The idea that imperfection can prove or proceed from perfection is further contradicted by the words of Jesus when he said, "<u>Even so, every good tree bringeth forth good fruit, but a corrupt tree bringeth forth evil fruit. A good tree cannot bring forth evil fruit, neither can a corrupt tree bring forth good fruit</u> (St. Matthew 17-18)." 'Abdu'l-Baha perhaps recognized this flaw in his reasoning and later reversed himself in his attempt to refute the evolutionary modification of species, for he states:

"For all existing beings, terrestrial and celestial, as well as this limitless space and all that is in it, have been created and organized, composed, arranged and perfected as they ought to be; *the universe has no imperfection*, so that if all beings became pure intelligence and reflected forever and ever, it is impossible that they could imagine anything better than that which exists (SAQ pg. 177, 'Abdu'l-Baha)."

Well, I do not know about you, dear reader, but my imagination is a bit more creative. It is clear the passages above directly contradict one another and cancel each other out. Furthermore, "if all beings became pure intelligence," wouldn't that be something better than what exist now? Let us proceed, however, to examine how the "imperfections of the contingent world" allegedly prove "the perfections of God."

"For example, when you look at man, you see that he is weak. This very weakness of the creature is a proof of the power of the **Eternal Almighty One**, because, if there were no power, weakness could not be imagined (SAQ pg. 5, 'Abdu'l-Baha)."

The above passage is a non sequitur. Although weakness can only be comprehended in contrast to strength, this fact does not imply or prove the existence of an "Eternal Almighty One." All that is needed to discover and understand the variations of strength and weakness is to observe these distinctions within one's own species, between different species, or with regard to one's own abilities and failings.

***

For example, you see one man who has gone

to great lengths to build-up his muscles and he is strong, while another man has not worked toward this goal and he is skinny and weak; or you observe an elephant and perceive he is stronger than any man and every man is weak by comparison; or you discover you are mighty enough to lift a hundred pounds, but too weak to lift a thousand. In each of these cases, both weakness and strength are understood without the need of any "supreme being."

'Abdu'l-Baha, however, continues this line of reasoning with several different pairs of opposites: poverty vs. wealth; ignorance vs. knowledge; dependency vs. independence; illness vs. health. In every one of these examples his conclusion is the same: These opposing conditions prove the existence of an "Eternal Almighty One." As we have seen, however, this reasoning proves nothing of the sort and further consideration renders "God" unnecessary to the understanding of these conditions.

***

'Abdu'l-Baha refers to his "God" as the "*Eternal Almighty One* (SAQ pg. 5, 'Abdu'l-Baha)," he also states that, "Knowledge is an essential necessity of God and is inseparable from Him (SAQ pg. 171 'Abdu'l-Baha)." But later he says, "As each globe (planet, sun, star[20]) has a beginning, necessarily it has an end because every composition, collective or particular, must of necessity be decomposed. The only difference is that some are quickly decomposed, and others more slowly, but *it is*

---

[20]   Parenthesis mine.

impossible *that* *a* *composed* *thing* *should* *not*
eventually *be* *decomposed* (SAQ pg. 181
'Abdu'l-Baha)."

It is established, the ability to persist without
end can only be expressed by an indivisible
object (a super-solid), while knowledge is
possible only to compound existents, doomed
to decomposition, because knowledge itself is
a compound dynamic. Omniscience and
perpetuity can not be united because they are
mutually exclusive in nature. Therefore, there
is no "God."

***

The most absurd and erroneous topic in
"Some Answered Questions" is titled, "The
Non-existence of Evil" where 'Abdu'l-Baha
blindly and ignorantly asserts, "...Good

exists; evil is nonexistent" (SAQ pg. 264). He completely omits the very real evils which men do to themselves and others: such as murder, rape, torture, theft, lying, physical and mental abuse, occasional cannibalism and war.

Least we believe these are merely human failings, consider the following: some species of ants practice slavery; many animals bully and steal from members of their own species; ants and chimpanzees wage war against their own; hamsters, alligators, chimpanzees and lions will sometimes kill and eat their own kind (often it is the young which are devoured). In short, there are plenty of real evils in both nature and man.

***

Now that we have disproved both "God's" existence and 'Abdu'l-Baha's acquired infallibility, let us examine one more pseudo, intellectual argument, the immortality of the human spirit (whatever that is):

"The logical proof of the immortality of the spirit is this, that no sign can come from a non-existing thing -- that is to say, it is impossible that from absolute nonexistence signs should appear -- for the signs are the consequence of an existence, and the consequence depends upon the existence of the principle[21]. So from a non-existing sun no light can radiate: from a non-existing sea no waves appear; from a non-existing cloud no rain falls; a non-existing tree yields no fruit; a non-existing man neither manifests nor

---

[21] The writings become the principle, the followers are the cause, and the Kingdom their effect.

produces anything. Therefore, as long as signs of existence appear, they are a proof that the possessor of the sign is existent.

"Consider that today the Kingdom of Christ exists. From a non-existing king how could such a great kingdom be manifested? How, from a non-existing sea, can the waves mount so high? From a non-existing garden, how can such fragrant breezes be wafted? Reflect that no effect, no trace, no influence remains of any being after its members are dispersed and its elements are decomposed, whether it be a mineral, a vegetable or an animal. There is only the human reality and the spirit of man which, after the disintegration of the members, dispersing of the particles, and the destruction of the composition, persists and continues to act and to have power (SAQ pg. 225, 'Abdu'l-Baha)."

The preceding passage is almost entirely nonsense. A man is not a sun, or a sea, or a cloud, or a tree, and these things have very little in common with one. They cannot think or feel, imagine or reason, count, read, write, or communicate across the ages. Nor can they create computers, build skyscrapers, form governments, found philosophies, or combine information and experience to achieve wisdom.

It is apparent that the kingdom of Christ, consists of four gospels, plus the letters of the New Testament; the people who believe in, and are inspired by them; along with the buildings erected in his name. The dominion of Christ is maintained by the love and actions of the living, not by any magical influence from the dead.

Not only do the prophets of great religions attain this kind of immortality, but also the famous and wealthy, the expressive and inventive, the infamous and the cruel. It is because people know their works and deeds that their influence continues long after their deaths.

Among such immortals are intellectual giants Socrates, Plato, Aristotle, Benjamin Franklin, Thomas Jefferson, Ayn Rand, etc. This is not a matter of the perpetuity of any spiritual essence, but the influence of history, language, writing, invention and inspiration[22].

This persistence of influence, however,

---

[22]   In Hinduism there is a sacred mystery which says that if one is killed by a "god" one becomes immortal. To the atheist this puzzle is easily solved. The immortality obtained is not of a spiritual or ghostly nature, but intellectual. It is the persistence of the hero/"god's" epic which bestows immortality upon all the story's characters.

is only for the few. Billions shall pass-away without leaving a single trace of the lives they once led.

LET'S GET THE "GOD" OUT

"...One nation, indivisible, with liberty and justice for all."

In our Constitution there are two clauses establishing a separation of church and state. The first, that no religious test for office shall be required (USC[23] Article 6, section 3), the second forbidding Congress from making any law respecting (honoring or deferring to) an establishment of religion, or prohibiting the

---

[23]   United States Constitution

free exercise thereof (USC First Amendment).

Despite these clear passages, the United States' coins all bare the motto of "In God We Trust," and at the end of each President's oath of office, every President since George Washington, has uttered the phrase, "So help me God."

Additionally, the Pledge of Allegiance was modified from its original wording to include the phrase, "Under God."

Finally, the Christian holy days of Christmas and Easter have been established as Federal holidays.

With respect to our money, "In God We Trust" is a declaration of faith and, therefore, an establishment of religion. What business does the Federal government have to issue such a declaration? The answer is none, and it should be done away with[24]. The recent Presidential coins may be just such an attempt, as the motto, "In God We Trust" is stamped on the edge of these coins where few will see.

Regarding the Presidential oath of office, it would be more inclusive (of both the people and whatever "God" might exist) if the

---

[24]   Personally, I would like to see it replaced by a real American motto, namely, "Don't tread on me."

President ended his swearing-in with the phrase "So help me all," or "So help us all."

The Pledge of Allegiance should be returned to its original state without the "Under God" phrase and its declaration of faith upon all Americans.

Finally, the Christian holy days of Christmas and Easter should be dropped from the roll of Federal holidays and replaced by the Winter Solstice and Spring Equinox, which were celebrated the world over before the advent of Christendom.

Many Christians should welcome this chance to purify their faith, as more than a few no longer believe their savior was born in the Winter or arose from the grave on a Sunday.

NOBODY'S PERFECT

With the existence of "God" disproved, so too are all claims of prophethood, revelation and divinity nullified. Nevertheless, the founders of the world's great religions can still be measured and judged for what they really were, philosophers. Their creeds and examples are now subject to the examination and judgment of reason.

Although there are many more religions and religion founders than the ones to be examined here, these four (Baha'u'llah, Mohammad, Jesus, Moses)[25]have something special in common. They all claim to be

---

[25]

descended from the line of Abraham, whom they all consider a prophet.

Now this is interesting, because while "God" made promises and prophecies to him, we have no record of any teaching being given by Abraham to anyone, nor did he establish any kind of social order for men to live by. The only "teaching" anyone can claim from Abraham is the worship of Yahweh and the rite of circumcision[26].

---

[26]   I've always wondered just what the ancient Jews did with the foreskin after they cut it off. It is a form of human sacrifice, so maybe they burnt it on the alter, or perhaps they disposed of it as medical waste, or did they fry it up and eat it as a special snack, they could even have thrown it out for the dogs and birds to feast upon. Might they have possibly made wallets of them (Bwhahahaha…)? The Bible just does not say.

'Abdu'l-Baha said (in reference to founding "prophets" called Manifestations of "God"), "...he must be at the same time their material and human as well as their spiritual educator--that is to say, he must teach men to organize and carry out physical matters, and to form a social order to establish cooperation and mutual aid in living so that material affairs may be organized and regulated for any circumstances that may occur (SAQ pg. 9, 'Abdu'l-Baha)."

Just how many of these "Manifestations Of 'God'" measure up to this description? Among those which concern us here, only Moses and Baha'u'llah devised any structured social order. Jesus promoted no integrated social design and left such matters entirely to his followers. The same is true of Mohammad.

Another thing all these founding

"prophets" have in common is hatred toward "idol worshipers." But people do not worship idols, and they rarely ever have. An idol is just an aid to prayer, to remind the supplicant of "God's" many attributes. It's just a symbol like the cross.

Furthermore, the Jews, Muslims, and Baha'is all have what is known as a point of adoration. A direction, a place, and/or a structure toward which they face for prayer. The Jews have Jerusalem and the wailing wall, Muslims have the Kaaba, Baha'is have the Shrine of Baha'u'llah in Bahji, Israel near Acre.

Whether it is a statue, a corpse, or a shrine makes no real difference, they serve the same purpose and any may be regarded as an idol. Jesus, however, rejected the use of a point of adoration:

"Woman, believe me, the hour cometh, when ye shall neither in this mountain, nor yet at Jerusalem, worship the Father. . . . . God is a Spirit: and they that worship him must worship him in spirit and in truth (St. John 21 & 24)."

**

Baha'u'llah, devised his vision of a future world order around the following ideals: the oneness of mankind, the oneness of religion, the independent investigation of truth, the abandonment of prejudice and superstition, universal compulsory education, equality of men and women, adoption of an inter-national auxiliary language, the harmony of religion and science, economic principles requiring work for all and the abolition of extremes of poverty and wealth, a universal house of justice, a world tribunal, and universal peace. While most of these are lofty goals in theory, their implementation falls far short of their potential.

Mankind's oneness is a no brainer and presents no problem as an ideal. It has, in principle, been accepted the world over. The oneness of religion, however, is bogus as all the religions express certain fundamental and irreconcilable differences.

The independent investigation of truth, is not the life long journey that it should be, but merely a path to the Baha'i Faith. Upon reaching this goal, a Baha'i is expected to abandon this search except within the confines of the Faith.

Abandoning prejudice and superstition are praiseworthy aims, but every religion contains its own prejudices, which are stagnate within each creed, and there is nothing really to distinguish religion from superstition. In fact, all religion is superstition, as the majority of any doctrine is unproven.

"When you believe in things that you do not understand Then you suffer. Superstition ain't the way, yeah, yeah" (Stevie Wonder, "Very Superstitious")

Universal, compulsory education has already been achieved in every civilized part of the world, but it has its problems too. Its primary problem comes from its being compulsory. Nobody likes to be forced into anything, and the natural reaction to compulsion is resistance.

This often takes the form of refusing to pay attention in class, not doing assigned homework, not participating in class, harassing other students, playing hooky, and even murdering teachers and classmates.

A different attitude must be encouraged and reflected throughout. The student must be encouraged to embrace its education, not as something the pupil must do, but as something it gets to do.

It is, however, the principle of the equality of men and women where the Baha'i Faith fails most noticeably. Men and woman are considered equal in every essential respect except for two. Women may not serve on the Universal House Of Justice[8] and homosexuality is prohibited. So women are still viewed as inferior to men and neither sex is equal to the other in seeking a marital partner. Women do not share with men the right to marry women and men do not share with women the right to marry men. This reality is shared with all the faiths being discussed here.

With respect to the adoption of an

---

[8]   Many Baha'is were so disconcerted by this inconsistency, regarding the equality of men and women, that their Universal House Of Justice put out a statement saying that they may have found a way for women to serve on the supreme governing body. I do not know what the result of this investigation was, however.

international auxiliary language[9], the world already has one. It's called English and it has become the auxiliary language of the world because it is the language of the dominate trade power, the United States of America.

Because of this, English is taught all over the Earth, often as a mandatory class. If it remains the dominate trade language long enough, it will eventually become the only tongue throughout the world. It is a waste of time and resources to teach everyone two languages when one common speech will do.

The harmony of religion and science is a

---

[9]   If "God" has decided that mankind should be able to communicate through a common language, then it is quite a change from the "God"/"gods" that confused the common language of those working on the so-called tower of Babel.

farce. Religion depends on revelation and blind faith. Science relies on reason, observation, and experimentation. These two approaches to knowledge and truth will never be compatible. Philosophy, on the other hand, can be wed to science, especially the philosophy of Ayn Rand.

Economic principles requiring work for all and the abolition of extremes of poverty and wealth, sound very much like the communist slogan, **"From each according to their ability, to each according to their need,"** which has been proved to be a destructive economic model. It is no more likely to succeed with a religious element than it has been alone.

As for a universal house of justice, a

world tribunal, and universal peace, a universal house of justice would be a world tribunal, and we have one now. It's called the United Nations. They only try the leaders of nations and such, they do not ever try the common man or crimes at that level. As for universal peace, we will not have that until the people of the Middle East stop fighting each other.

In his attempt to make a compromise between arranged marriages and allowing people to freely choose their own marital partners, Baha'u'llah, purposed that individuals should select their potential spouses, but then seek the approval of the parents on both sides. If any parent disapproves, then the wedding is off. This is no concession at all. If parents can nullify their child's choice, then parents might just as well pick their child's spouse in the first place.

***

All these founding, religious philosophers gave special importance to the act of prayer. However, they and their followers differ as to exactly how, when and where one should pray and what to ask for. The real purpose of prayer, however, is to teach a believer humility, dependence, and discipline. As for the form of prayer, Baha'u'llah liked to devise lengthy calls and addresses to the "Deity." Jesus expressed the opposite view:

"But when ye pray, use not vain repetitions,

as the heathen do: for they think that they shall be heard for their much speaking (St. Matthew 6, 7)."

What Mohammad had to do with it I do not know, but the Muslims pray in public in huge masses. Jesus told his followers not to pray in public, not even in the church,

"And when thou prayest, thou shalt not be as the hypocrites are: for they love to pray standing in the synagogues and in the corners of the streets, that they may be seen of man. Verily I say unto you, they have their reward.

". . . . when thou prayest, enter into thy closet and when thou hast shut thy door, pray to thy Father which is in secret and thy Father which sees in secret will reward you openly (St. Mathew 6:5-6)."

***

The Koran is filled with stories about many of

the same events which are found in the Judeo-Christian Bible, but the stories are very different from their telling in the Bible. The story of Christ's birth, for example, is very different. In it, Mary gives birth to Jesus beneath a tree.

Either the Koran, the Bible, or both must be wrong, if both are intended literally. The greatest thing Muhammad achieved was to put an end to the barbaric, practice of burying first born daughters alive in the sand.

Jesus is perhaps best known for his beatitudes, but his faults are unknown to the average Christian. For example, while he warned men against calling others names like Raca and fool, he called all non Jews dogs:

But he answered and said, "It is not meet to take the children's (the Jews') bread, and to cast it to dogs (gentiles) (Matthew 15:26)."

He had other names for different people. He called the Pharisees vipers, and so forth. This alone shows him to have been a leader/teacher that didn't care enough about setting a good example to follow his own advice.

Mohammad was just as bad. When asked why he took four wives but only allowed his followers two, he is reported to have said, **"He that makes the rules can brake the rules."**

***

When Jesus was asked if it was lawful for the Jews to pay a certain tax (St. Matt 22:17-22), he asked whose image was stamped on the coin. Once he was told the coin bore the likeness of Caesar, Jesus replied, "Give unto Caesar that which is Caesar's and unto God, that which is God's."

Although this response is open to all kinds of interpretation, the person left out of this exchange was the poor slob who had to break his back, for that small coin, just to feed his family. Between Caesar and "God," what portion might the working man claim as his own? Jesus offered him none.

Jesus is said to have healed many people of many different ailments: blindness, muteness, a lame man or two, leprosy. But as the son of "God," surely Jesus could have taught people how to purify their water for drinking, without having to turn it into alcohol.

It's really not that hard, but it's a practical thing which would have saved a lot of lives. He could have taught them logic, the basics of medicine, etc. But no, he didn't. It took us nearly two thousand years to cure leprosy, but we did it. We achieved it because of Greek philosophy.

There was also that thing with the fig tree (St. Mark 11:12-21). Jesus saw it in the distance and he was hungry. Well it wasn't the season for fig trees to bare their fruit, but that didn't stop Jesus. He walked right up to it and, seeing it bore no fruit, he cursed the poor hapless tree. The next day the tree was dead. Now was that reasonable, expecting a tree to bare fruit out of season and blaming the tree for his disappointment?

Jesus also said a house divided against itself cannot stand (St. Luke 11:17) and yet, was there ever anything so splintered and set against itself as Christendom? How many different flavors of the one true faith? Not so many as stars in the sky, but quite a lot. Yet this house shows no sign of collapsing any day soon.

To judge a man by his fruits (St. Matt 7:16) is what Jesus admonished, so let him be judged by his. What have the fruits of Christendom been? Religious wars, witch trials, intellectual decay, superstition, ignorance, etc., the fruit of an evil tree. And yet, his followers acknowledge only the good.

***

Moses was the leader of the Hebrew nation during its slavery in Egypt and after its liberation, but what were they liberated from? Was it bondage, slavery, a tyrannical pharaoh? Yes, from all these things were the Jewish people freed. But what were they released to: a tyrannical "holy" man, whose law contained far too many death penalty offenses (Lev 20:9-27).

One could be stoned to death for using the "Lord's" name in vain, for disrespecting one's parents, or for marrying a foreigner, to name just a few. The problem with so many death sentences is that if you commit one such offense, you might as well commit them all. You're going to die anyway and you can only be killed once.

When the same punishment is prescribed for a variety of offenses, those crimes are rendered equal by the effect of the law. So, with respect to Mosaic law, each of the following offences are equal in that the penalty for each is death: being a rude, disobedient, or disrespectful child, taking the name of Yahweh in vain, to wrought confusion, murder, rape, adultery, homosexuality, fornication, bestiality (a lot of these are sexual in nature).

This all means that, under the law, a disrespectful child is no better than a murderer or a rapist, and they are no worse than the child. In fact, no offender of this list is any better than a murderer or rapist, as every one of them is equal to every other, under the law.

Even taking the "LORD's" name in vain is no worse than engaging in bestiality (under this code), and no better than being gay. Clearly this is an excessive and bizarre code of "justice."

Things are much better today. Our laws are much more reasonable now and so are the penalties for breaking them.

In America, and the West, only murderers are commonly executed, everyone else receives prison time and/or fines. It is logic that rules the courts now and reason which sets the punishment given each offense.

SOME OBSERVATIONS

The Judeo-Christian bible is a remarkable collection of writings, some of which are more than three thousand years old. They have survived many threats to their existence, including censorship, and war. Too bad the Bible has never been translated literally. **"In the beginning God created the heavens and the earth"** is perhaps the best known verse in the whole Bible. And this is where the mistranslations begin.

The word "God," in the quote above, is actually translated from the Hebrew word elohim, which is plural, "gods" not "God." I've also been told elohim is feminine, so it could be translated, **"In the beginning the *grand matriarchs* created the heavens and the earth."** Or it could be translated as, **"In the beginning the *mighty ones* created the heavens and the earth,"** or **"In the beginning the *gods* created the heavens and the earth."** Every time you see the word God in this first chapter, any of the above are possible. It's another story in chapter two.

Chapter one offers us an orderly account of the creation, and on the sixth day man and woman are created. But chapter two is very different. The earth is barren and nothing grows on it, because there is no man to tend it. So the "Lord God" makes Adam out of the dust of the ground. Just as "God" is a mistranslation in chapter one, so is the phrase "Lord God" in chapter two. This phrase is substituted for the proper name of the Hebrew "God," Yahweh is the best guess among scholars.

At its beginning, the Hebrew alphabet had no vowel markings. The vowel sounds were passed on orally. The Hebrew "God's" real name was never spoken out of the fear "God" would smite anyone who might misuse it. After a while, the pronunciation was lost and no body knew how to say it anymore.

Whenever the word spirit appears anywhere in the Bible, it is translated -- incorrectly -- from one of four words meaning wind or breath. Also, there is no word for mind in the original languages of the Old

Testament. Every time you see the word mind, it has been interpreted and translated from words meaning breath, wind, or heart.

Furthermore, the Old and New Testaments differ on the meaning of the word soul. In the early Hebrew texts, a soul is any living being. In the later texts, a soul is something everyone has.

***

Next Yahweh creates a wonderful garden, in which He places Adam. After some time has passed, Yahweh notices it is not good for Adam to be alone, so Yahweh proceeds to create the animals, which He shows to Adam so he may name them. Well, Adam doesn't find a suitable companion among the animals, so Yahweh decides to make a woman.

Yahweh causes Adam to fall into a deep sleep and takes one of his ribs and creates a woman from it for Adam. When Adam awakes, he meets the woman and names her Eve.

Now this all makes Yahweh sound pretty stupid. One would think a "god" would know Adam was going to feel lonely before making him. "It" would also know to make woman from the beginning, before the animals, but Yahweh doesn't seem to have much foresight or intelligence.

Many Christians, Jews and Muslims believe "God" made everything out of nothing. And while the first creation story might seem to support such a position, the second creation story does not. Yahweh, makes the plants, animals, and Adam out of the dust of the ground.

This "god" requires pre-existing materials from which to make things. Eve was made out of Adam's rib. This story depicts a "god" which exists, not above or beyond, but within nature.

Yahweh, placed a special tree in the middle of Eden, the tree of the knowledge of good and evil, which He told Adam not to eat of least he die. Eve, however, ate from the forbidden tree and gave some to Adam who did eat as well. For this infraction, Yahweh expelled them from the garden, but first He killed some animals and made the disobedient pair some clothes.

Sometime later, Adam and Eve have sex and Eve bears their first son, Cain. The next child Eve birthed was Able. In the fullness of time, each brother made an offering to Yahweh, Cain from the fruits of the earth and Able from his flock of sheep. Yahweh showed Able and his offering respect, but He showed no respect to Cain or his offering. This made Cain very angry and jealous. Jealous of his brother's success and angry at Yahweh.

Later, Cain argues with his brother and kills him. He buries Able's body in the sand. Yahweh confronts Cain about his missing brother and discovers Cain slew Able. Yahweh curses Cain to be a wanderer and a beggar. Cain protest his punishment is too great and anyone who finds him will kill him.

Yahweh places a mark of protection on Cain's brow and hands and declares he shall be avenged seven times should anyone kill him, and this is the beginning of man's doom because Yahweh decided to protect a murderer.

With Yahweh's protective marks on his hands and forehead, Cain runs from the face of Yahweh (which I take to indicate Yahweh was just a local deity) and goes to the land of Nod. There he finds a wife (either Yahweh made other people in different locations, or the "gods" of chapter one did, otherwise how could Cain find a wife in a foreign land), has a son, and builds a city. Doesn't seem like Yahweh's cruse had any real effect on Cain.

Many years later Lamech (a descendent

of Cain) brags to his wives that he has killed a young man and, because Yahweh protected Cain, if he is killed, he would be avenged seventy-seven times. So, murder has become something to brag about and be proud of. Mankind slips rapidly into decay after this.

Some time later, Yahweh observes that the wickedness of humanity was great in the Earth, and every imagination of the thoughts of its heart was only evil continually (Gee, I wonder why). So, Yahweh decides to destroy every person on the Earth except for Noah, his household and his floating zoo.

After the flood has come and gone, Yahweh announces **"Whoso sheddeth man's blood, by man shall his blood be shed: for in the image of Yahweh made**

He man (Genesis 9:6)." And so, the wickedness of man is shown to be Yahweh's fault for protecting a murderer and not enforcing his curse upon Cain.

The Bible is not a good source for factual knowledge, for it describes the Sun as traveling around the Earth, **"The Sun also ariseth, and the Sun goeth down, and hasteth to his place where he arose** (Ecclesiastes 1:5)." We all know the Bible is wrong about this. There are other errors throughout, but we will not be exploring those.

It is a curious thing that Adam and Eve ate of the fruit of the tree of the knowledge of good and evil, and yet their descendents were in need of the ten commandments later. Did the effects of the fruit wear off or something? This fruit condemned the entire human race to eventual death, regardless of anyone's power of choice.

Yet, when Jesus died on the cross, his sacrifice wasn't great enough to cancel original sin for the whole human race without regard for anyone's choice. His sacrifice has to be acknowledged and its effects requested.

***

When the ten commandments were given, the second one read, **"Thou shalt not make thee any graven image, or any likeness of any thing that is in heaven above, or that is in the earth beneath, or that is in the waters beneath the earth: Thou shalt not bow down thyself unto them, nor serve them: for I the Lord thy God am a jealous God, visiting the iniquity of the fathers upon the children unto the third and fourth generation of**

them that hate me (Deuteronomy 5:6-21)."

Yet, when the children of Israel were instructed on the building of the Ark of the Covenant they were told to place two cherubim (a kind of angel), one on each end of the Ark (Exodus 25:18-20). Is this not a contradiction of the second commandment?

The second commandment also states that **"God" visits "the iniquity of the fathers upon the children unto the third and fourth generation of them that hate me."** But this is contradicted in Jeremiah 31:29-30 and Ezekiel 18:1-32, both of which say a man is accountable for his own transgressions and he will be judged on his own merits.

If I told you to tell a lie for me, and you did so, would I not be as guilty of the lie as you? Of course I would be. Well, this is just what Yahweh does when he wants to kill a particular king. Yahweh sends a certain spirit to put a lying tongue into the mouths of all the king's prophets, so he will be encouraged to make war on his neighbor and be killed.

Why Yahweh doesn't just zap the king with a bolt from the blue, we will never know, but "god" just doesn't (I Kings 22:19-22). This puts a lie to the verse which says, **"God is not a man, that he should lie; . . .** (Numbers 23:19)."

***

Although it was prohibited under the laws of Moses and Christianity later, there is evidence King David was at least bisexual as a young man. Following the battle in which King Saul and his sons died, David expresses this lament over Jonathan, one of King Saul's sons, *"I am distressed for you, my brother Jonathan; you were very dear to me; your love to me was wonderful, <u>passing</u> <u>the</u> <u>love</u> <u>of</u> <u>women</u>* (2 Samuel 1:26)."

Now some might object saying David and Jonathan were just very close friends, but why compare his love to that of women unless it was sexual, as this is the chief distinction between the love a man might commonly share with another, and that which a woman might provide?

The Mythology Of The Devil

Perhaps the most interesting character in the Bible is "God's" archenemy the Devil. Whether we call him the Devil, Satan, or Lucifer, he is the fallen angel who challenged Yahweh, and tempted Eve to sin. As Lucifer he is the bringer of light (knowledge), and the most beautiful and perfect thing in heaven, excepting "God."

Lucifer can be compared to Prometheus (the Greek "god" of foresight) who brought humanity fire, light and knowledge. Satan, by tempting Eve to sin, also gave man the gift of knowledge. However, the story of Lucifer, an angel who rebelled against the "Almighty," makes no sense.

"God" is suppose to be a perfect being, so everything Yahweh made would have been perfect also: the sands, the seas, angels and men would exist without defect. Lucifer would have been completely content, in a perfect heaven. So, heaven could not have been so grand. If heaven is flawed, then so is its creator.

So, perhaps we should look at the Lucifer character in a new light, maybe even as a hero. Prometheus was punished for giving man fire by being chained to a rock where a great vulture came and ate his liver every day. At night his liver would grow back again. Satan has yet to be punished for opening our eyes.

Now the New Testament calls the Devil

the father of lies (John 8:44), but if you look at the scriptures you will not find a single instance where the Devil was less than truthful. Take the garden of Eden and the tempting of Eve. The Devil, disguised as a serpent, told Eve that if she ate from the tree of the knowledge of good and evil she would become like "God."

Well, this was no lie. It is actually confirmed by Yahweh, himself, "And the LORD God (Yahweh) said, Behold, the man is become as one of us, to know good and evil: and now, lest he put forth his hand, and take also from the tree of life, and eat, and live forever...."

AN EPISTLE TO MOM

So, you do not like it when I use the Bible to expose the contradictions and errors therein. Can you offer me a better standard from which to analyze and judge your religious tome? If you can, I will be quite willing, even happy, to re-evaluate my position relative to your faith (religion). Personally, I prefer to employ the standard of reason and logical analysis. By this means, I have already discovered a unique proof (if one is open to the possibility of proof) explaining why "God" does not and cannot exist as any of the world's religions describe or conceive "It."

If, on the other hand, one is the type of

person who responds to a challenge by sticking their fingers in their ears and singing, "Blah, blah, blah. I am not listening. Blah, blah, blah," then no proof is possible. Nor is such a person worthy of the effort (the old pearls before swine thing).

***

The last time I visited, you claimed that you had shown your children the path and now it was up to them to embrace it or not, that you had done your part. With respect to promoting your own creed, this is mostly untrue.

It was Dad, and not you, who regularly read to us from our children's Bible, a heavily edited and condensed version of the "holy" writ. All you ever did, in this regard, was to take us to church where the preacher would attend to our "spiritual" education, not you.

Regardless of who provided the indoctrination, the effects on me were terrible nightmares about the judgment day and the end of the world in which sometimes I was among the saved, sitting on the right hand of "God" and other times I was assigned to join the damned.

Every night I went to sleep facing the wall, in order to catch the Devil should he attempt to sneak-up on me by slipping through. But worse of all were the times when you left me alone at home, for more than thirty minutes, during a thunder storm, and I would become very frightened, imagining the rapture had come and left me alone on the Earth.

I was constantly filled with emotions of guilt and doubt. I was always more spiritually minded than you, even confronting you on your "taking the 'LORD's' name in vain."

***

Your complete lack of interest (more like a stubborn refusal) in either checking my references against my claims, or in offering well-reasoned counterpoints of your own, indicates the following: you do not love me (otherwise you would be devoted to getting my head in the right place for me to return to the fold), you know you would be outgunned and out classed in an actual, intellectual discussion (so you will not even try), you're afraid you might actually learn a thing or two, you can not stand the notion that your daddy was wrong and passed faulty information to you (I am sure he wasn't aware of his error), you can not accept the fact that there might not be any heaven in which you would re-unite with your second husband and other lost, loved ones (dust is dust and dead is dead).

You've told me many times, "There are none so blind as will not see." I would like to add, "There are none so deaf as will not hear, and none so ignorant as will not think."

Your general attitude appears to be something along the line that, because you once followed the directions in the book of Romans, "If thou shalt confess with thy mouth the Lord Jesus, and shalt believe in thine heart that God has raised him from the dead, thou shalt be saved," you are forever saved and there is nothing more that you need do to secure your salvation.

***

You have said, on several occasions, that you may not have any jewels in your crown, in heaven, but at least you will still be there. If I were you, I would really reconsider this position, because the Bible doesn't support it at all. Jesus, himself had other ideas:

"<u>And</u> <u>everyone</u> <u>that</u> <u>hearth</u> <u>these</u> <u>sayings</u> <u>of</u> <u>mine,</u> <u>and</u> <u>doeth them not</u>, shall be likened unto a foolish man, which built his house upon the sand:

"And the rain descended, and the floods came, and the winds blew, and beat upon that house; and it fell: and great was the fall of it (Matthew 7:26-27)." Furthermore, "Not everyone that saith unto me Lord, Lord, shall enter into the kingdom of heaven; but he that doeth the will of my Father which is in heaven.

"Many will say to me in that day, Lord, Lord, have we not prophesied in thy name? and in thy name have cast out devils? and in thy name done many wonderful works?

"And then will I profess unto them, I never knew you: depart from me, ye that work iniquity (Matthew 7:21-23)."

And moreover, "Then shall he also say unto them on the left hand, depart from me, ye cursed, into everlasting fire, prepared for the devil and his angles.

"For I was an hungered, and ye gave me no meat: I was thirsty, and ye gave me no drink:

"I was a stranger, and you took me not in: naked, and ye clothed me not sick, and in prison, and ye visited me not.

"Then shall he answer them, saying, Verily I say unto you, In as much as ye did it not to one of the least of these, ye did it not to me.

"...And these shall go away into

everlasting punishment: but the righteous into life eternal, (Matthew 25:41-43, 45-46)."

In the book of Acts there is a story of how and why a certain couple lost their salvation. This story begins at Acts 5:34-37. It is explained that the early Christian community would sell their possessions and then give the proceeds to the Apostles to be redistributed following the Marxist formula of, "From each according to their ability, to each according to their need."

Anyway, there was this couple that decided they wanted to make a very large contribution, without actually giving it all up. Well, this didn't go over too well with the Apostles or their "God." They accused the couple, first the man and then his wife, of lying to the Holy Spirit. Each, in their turn, dropped dead on the spot after being exposed. Somehow, I do not think either of these two went to heaven.

***

Jesus is often referred to as the "son of 'God,'" but he is not the only one to carry this title. Adam, the first progenitor of Christ, is also called the "son of 'God,'" (St. Luke 3:38) as are the angles (Genesis 6:2 & Job 1:6). Furthermore, all of Jesus' followers are given the power to become the "sons of 'God'" as well (John 1:12).

If being a "son of 'God'" makes one of the same substance with "God," as the doctrine of the Trinity asserts -- a doctrine that is neither described or explained anywhere in the Bible, then what exists within the Godhead, is not a trinity, but a divine multiplicity.

*****

Personally, I really do not care how badly people misinterpret and twist the "scriptures" they claim to follow and revere. I have no respect for anyone's religion, but I do rather enjoy examining the verities and such of mythology, and the lessons it is employed to teach. At best, Jesus is just a religious philosopher, to me.

*****

Now if the Jehovah's Witnesses have the correct understanding of Christian mythology, as described in scripture, and Jesus is actually the incarnation of the arch angle Michael, then Lucifer would be a brother to

Jesus and a "son of 'God,'" himself. The Nicene Creed (325CE) may use the phrase, "God the Father, God the Son, and God the Holy Ghost," but it does not appear anywhere in the Judeo-Christian bible.

On several occasions, Jesus says that he is one with the Father and such statements are commonly used to lend support to the doctrine of the trinity, but this is an unlikely meaning, because Jesus repeatedly refers to the Father as having superior position and authority to and over himself.

On several occasions, Jesus says that he is one with the Father and such statements are commonly used to lend support to the doctrine of the trinity, but this is an unlikely meaning, because Jesus repeatedly refers to the Father as having superior position and authority to and over himself.

If Jesus were actually "God the son," it would be pointless for Jesus to pray to the Father to release him from the sacrifice of his mortal life on the cross. He could have simply excused himself on his own authority.

A clue to the meaning of Christ's oneness with "God" can be discovered in one of his prayers to his Father. At St. John 17, Jesus prays to his Father, asking repeatedly that his disciples, and all their converts should be one, _even as Jesus is one with "God_." And that they should be one with Jesus and also with "God." Moreover, that each should be within each. That all must be one.

Surely the disciples are not of one substance with "God," or with each other. No, this oneness can only mean that they are of one mind, one heart and/or one purpose. The apostles never merged into a single being. Being within each other just means to have influenced and been mindful of each other. Nowhere does the Bible state that anyone need believe or acknowledge the "Godhood" of Christ, in order to be saved.

The "son of 'God'" is not the only title that Jesus bore. He also referred to himself as the "son of man" (A prophetic title used by many of the Hebrew prophets), as such he forgave sins (Matthew 9:6); there is also his political claim as the "son of David."

***

While you had very little to do with promoting your own beliefs to me, or my siblings, you contributed to my own spiritual path a fair bit more. You introduced me to "Be Here Now" and Baba Ram Dass. Which lead me to the exploration of Buddhism, Hinduism, Taoism, and the practice of Eastern meditation.

Then you practically introduced me to that Christian cult, "The Way Ministry," without even inquiring as to what they believed. This group is where I was first exposed to the idea that Jesus isn't "God."

Another influence that came through you, was the book, "The Virtue of Selfishness" and its author, Ayn Rand, who promoted the idea of rational atheism. Her work really impressed me and had a defining influence several years later.

✳✳✳

With regard to your censoring my writings from my oldest niece, I am going to allow that you felt you were somehow protecting her from "spiritual" harm, but that does not explain your extreme reaction to just a few pages of philosophical analysis.

You were obviously afraid for your own sake, as well as for my niece's. If you had any real confidence in your own beliefs, you could have read it for yourself and remain unaffected, or you might have been inspired with some good counter-points which have persuade your oldest son to re-enter the fold. Five Catholics have already read what you destroyed. I doubt that they will leave the church because of it.

Well, I guess this pretty much sums things up for now. I will talk to you again later.

ATHEISM VS BUDDHISM

We all reach nirvana in the end, whether we chase after it or not. Each candle will be extinguished in its turn. Neither attachment nor desire will keep one's flame alight. So revel in the time that's yours.

Atheists, with rare exception, do not believe in an afterlife. We believe in the nothingness from which we came and to which everyone returns. The elder branch of Buddhism sought this same nothingness.

During their lifetimes, Gautama's followers practiced emotional detachment, so that, in death, each might obtained nirvana. They lived and struggled to achieve these states of mind and being. Such effort was considered necessary, by the Buddha, in order to escape the cycle of death and rebirth, otherwise the soul would be reincarnated.

Upon being reborn, the soul would again

suffer the pains of the world. To become nothing was considered a far better thing than to suffer the world's sorrows again and again and again...

Although detachment has its value, as a backdrop to life, the effort to achieve nirvana is unnecessary: the character, personality, or soul does not survive the death of its medium, the human brain. It's chemical encodings will dissolve and disperse, while its electric current will discharge. Likewise, will go the mind, to its own non-existence[27].

Because non-existence is absolute and

---

[27] Our existence is but a passing arrangement of particles, in an eternal sea of matter and energy; a transitory collection of neurons, hosting a finite mind, expressing limited thought and emotion.

unavoidable, atheists do not worry about pleasing any "God," to avoid fiery hell, or to get into heaven upon their deaths. Instead we revel, unafraid, in the time we have to live.

Atheism gives us comfort in our eventual dissolution, knowing it will bring the final end to all we are and were. Within the nothingness of non-existence, joy and sorrow, pleasure and pain, ignorance and knowledge, hope and despair, love and hate will all be made void and empty, and we shall be no more.

Siddhartha started his journey to find a means to escape the suffering of old age, illness and death. His solution centered around extinguishing all emotion. We atheists feel this is the wrong answer.

While it is good to develop a background of detachment, emotions are part of the rewards of life and living. Since life is truly temporary, why not enjoy all its pleasures, as long as you violate neither the property or person of another?

Sexuality

FROM THE SEEDS OF DESIRE
SPRINGS THE HARVEST OF LOVE

It is said that the quickest way to a man's heart is through his stomach. This is not so, Actually, the fastest way to any man's heart is by way of his groin.

The special advantage masturbation grants to the mindful practitioner is a position of strength in the pursuit of romantic relations. Being sexually sufficient within one's self, allows for a more relaxed and confident approach, as opposed to the desperate questing of those who are incomplete.

THE DAWN OF SEXUALITY

CLEARLY, THE BEST EXPLANATION for the development of cross-gender reproduction, or reproductive coupling, is the theory which suggests it evolved from bacterial cannibalization[28]. This theory is based on the fact that certain strains of bacteria will cannibalize, or extract, genetic material from deceased members of their own strain, in order to repair or improve their genetic code. These bacteria will also exchange genetic material with living members of their strain for the same purpose.

The connection between this behavior, in certain bacteria, and cross-gender reproduction is indicated by the fact that when egg and sperm unite, the first thing they do is to replicate their own genetic material, exchange parts of their codes and then continue the process of reproduction. A further fact supporting this theory, is that the purpose of reproductive coupling is the same as the goal of bacterial cannibalization. In both cases, the

---

[28]   "Eros And Evolution: A Natural Philosophy Of Sex" by Richard E. Michod

aim is to acquire the best genetic material.

Eventually, members within the same species came to differ with regard to gender -- one gender (the female) producing the egg, and the other (the male) the sperm. This distinction probably occurred after the development of multicelled organisms and specialized, reproductive cells.

EXISTENTIAL ENRICHMENT

Although sex has its origin in the reproductive drive, as the immediate motivation and reward for pro-creative coupling, its development as a means for the celebration of life and the most intensely intimate expression of friendship, admiration, affection, and love began with the advent of subjective consciousness and self-awareness about three thousand years ago[29].

The most important question for a being of subjective consciousness is whether life is worth living or not. Consequently, the most important emotional experience is the one which affirms life is indeed worthwhile.

Sex, as both the most intense celebration of life and as the most intimate expression of friendship, admiration, affection and love, is the ultimate psycho-physio-emotional affirmation of life's value. As such, sex is the product of the subjective mind's ability to recall the instances and circumstances of genital arousal and

---

[29]   "The Origin Of Consciousness In The Breakdown Of The Bicameral Mind" by Julian Jaynes Copyright 1976.

orgasmic release and to consider, project, imagine and pursue these occurrences.

Beyond the psycho-emotional benefits of sex, as the ultimate affirmation of life's value, sex also has many important physiological benefits which are well known. Among these are its ability to relive depression, tension and stress, block minor pain, temporarily alleviate respiratory congestion, promote appetite, improve general health and well-being and extend life itself.

Unlike many other values, however, the life-sustaining and enhancing benefits of sex are readily available to nearly everyone. There are, however, many obstacles to sexual fulfillment -- most of which are unnecessary and easily overcome.

One of the more significant impediments to sexual attainment stems from its connection to reproduction. Until recently, cross-gender sexual activity has always carried the risk of producing unwanted offspring. This fact had many negative consequences -- mostly for women and children.

Unintended children were often resented, feared, and mistreated by their unwilling parents. If a child were conceived out-of-wedlock, the pregnancy would sentence the woman to death as a fornicator. (The child would, of course, die unborn within its mother.) If the child were conceived in an act of adultery, however, its mother would suffer the same fate only if the child were too noticeably different, in appearance, from its father or siblings.

Often unwanted offspring were killed immediately after being born. Abortions could be induced through dangerous herbal concoctions and beatings -- either of which could result in the woman's death or her permanent sterility. Apart from these harsh realities, pregnancy itself was often a life-threatening condition.

Before the medical benefits of hand washing and the discovery of antibiotics, women frequently died during childbirth or from infection afterwards. For all these reasons, women had to be especially cautious in their pursuit of sexual fulfillment.

There were, of course, other avenues for the pursuit of sexual fulfillment, even before the advent of modern medicine and condoms. Unfortunately, most people were discouraged from pursuing them or punished if they did. This situation was due entirely to the religions and philosophies which dominated our ancestors through most of our history.

With rare exception, these religions and philosophies viewed sex as little more than a necessary evil and restricted sex to its role as the immediate motivation and reward for reproductive coupling. reproductive coupling, moreover, was confined by these systems of belief to the institution of marriage between a man and a woman or a man and several women. While there were certain reproductive advantages to this position, there were also many disadvantages as well.

On the plus side, confining sexual pleasure and reproduction to the institution of marriage helped to insure a woman would be provided for during her pregnancy and her offspring would not be immediately orphaned if she died following its birth. Punishing fornication (sex between unmarried people), frequently with execution, served to insure that these safeguards were in place before offspring were conceived.

Executing adulterers helped to protect a man from the hardship of involuntarily providing for children who were not his own. The prohibition against incest (sex between closely related people), helped to insure the infusion of fresh, and hopefully better, genes. It also served to prevent the occurrence of genetic defects which often follow after several generations of this practice.

On the minus side, this position leaves little room for love (the personal value one holds for another). Children were often viewed as the property of their parents. As such their parents decided whom they would wed. Parents were, of course, free to choose a partner their child showed affection for.

They were equally free, however, to choose their child's reproductive/sexual partner on the basis of genetic considerations, such as health, appearance or physical strength. They might also make their selection with regard to wealth, reputation, religious standing, political position or alliance, traditional affiliations, or friendships among families. A child's parents might also choose, or be obliged, to deny their child both progeny and sexual fulfillment.

A child might be given as an offering to a temple to serve as a celibate priest, priestess or the acolyte of some "god." If a child disagreed with its parents' choice of his wife, her husband, or temple, it was still the child's duty to honor the choice of its parents. This reality, however, often resulted in the child's resentment of its parents, the selected spouse or the temple. This frequently made for bad husbands, wives and a vindictive clergy.

The evolutionary advantage of cross-gender reproduction (having developed out of bacterial cannibalization) is inhibited by the institution of marriage -- especially monogamous marriage. In monogamous marriage, the selection for better genes is limited to only one candidate. This greatly slows the rate of genetic improvement among us.

Genetically speaking, it would be better if both men and women were free to continually pursue better genes. Polygamy limits the candidates to either one man or one woman (women have rarely been allowed this practice) and several opposite-gender partners.

The disdain these religious philosophies held for sex, moreover, produced the most damaging psychological effects. Their view of sex as a base emotional need deprived our ancestors of this most intense celebration of life. It transformed the metaphysical joy of sex into the condemnation of guilt, self-loathing, and shame.

Instead of the affirmation of life's supreme value, the condemnation of sex confirmed a sense of life's curse, a curse of constant misery. Life, in this view, was not a treasure to be cherished, it was a burden and a prison to be endured until the release of death.

These conditions were especially oppressive to women who were generally considered to be the property of their husbands with no rights, privileges, freedoms or properties of their own. It was considered a woman's lot in life to obey her husband without question and to submit to his every demand -- sexual or otherwise. A man could usually divorce his wife if she displeased him in some way, but a wife could never divorce her husband, not even if he beat or otherwise abused her.

Despite the misery of these circumstances, two groups actually thrived on this situation. Religious leaders and rulers depended on these dismal conditions for their support, power and wealth. Kings and clergy required a population of duty bound serfs, laborers, subjects and slaves to free them from the necessity of sustaining their lives through their own productive thought and labor.

By limiting sex to its role in reproductive coupling, they gained the growing population required to sustain their indolent lives. Also by condemning sexual pleasure as base, these parasites encouraged their victims to view their lot as a duty to be born with resignation and submission. Their condemnation also served to keep the population of their subjects from growing beyond their ability to maintain control.

The dependence of the non-working elite on the productive working class has always been the true reason behind the elite's condemnation of sex apart from reproductive coupling. It remains the primary motive behind their condemnation of condoms, the birth-control pill, abortion, masturbation, oral sex and homosexuality.

In order to impose this code of sexual/reproductive conduct, religious leaders, philosophers, and political authorities alike relied on the common desire for external authorization. To legitimize their authority they employed a remnant from past ages (before the development of subjective consciousness), when people were directed by auditory/visual hallucinations called "gods." (Such "gods" are most commonly experienced in modern times by those suffering from the mental illness known as schizophrenia.)

Unlike the hallucinated, earthly "gods" of the past, the "god(s)" of modern times are extra-dimensional and "heard" only by the self-appointed chosen. Such "gods" are imagined rather than hallucinated. They are products of the subjective mind and therefore, inferior to it. They have only the authority we ourselves give them.

We, however, are the masters of the things we imagine. The same priests and philosophers created the myth of an extra-dimensional, heavenly paradise in order to further persuade men to denounce the pleasure and happiness they might otherwise obtain for themselves in this world.

The subjective, conscious mind, however, has no need for the hallucinated "gods" of the past, the imaginary "gods" of an indolent elite or the directives of external authorization. All the subjective mind requires for guidance in its quest for meaning and fulfillment is the exercise of reason through the methods of observation and logic.

It is through the guidance of these means that we have discovered electricity, built skyscrapers, conquered diseases, exploded the atom and liberated sex from the service of reproduction.

Our subjective minds work by creating conceptual, analog models of ourselves, our world, our place in it and our relationships with others. This allows us to understand, examine and interact with the world around us in a way lesser animals cannot.

This form of consciousness gives us the ability to retain, conceive, consider, and expand our experience, behavior, identity and ideas in a way which transforms everything we perceive and encounter. It is the very nature of our minds which transforms sex beyond the immediate reward and motivation to breed into the embodiment and celebration of life and the most intimate expression of friendship, admiration, and love.

It is our profound need to celebrate the value of life and to experience the most intimate expression of friendship, admiration, and love which directs and propels our desire for sex beyond the production of offspring.

Sex so imbues us with the joy of living, so pervades our being with the emotional confirmation that life is worth living, worth the effort and struggle, that to deny or reject it is to profoundly diminish the value of our existence. To our most intimate and personal associations sex gives a sense of completion and fulfillment which would otherwise go unrealized and unachieved.

Reason affirms that the pursuit and achievement of happiness are essential to our survival and well-being. It is the promise of happiness and the experience of life-sustaining pleasure which motivates our productive/creative efforts and confirms our conviction that life is indeed worth living. The happiest individuals are often the most creative and productive.

Sex is a manifestation of happiness, an

expression of joy. As such, sex serves to provide the emotional fuel necessary for the continuous pursuit of life's sustenance. Sex best serves this purpose when indulged regularly apart from the propagation of children.

With the invention of the condom, in the eighteenth century, it became possible, for the first time, to both intentionally and consistently liberate cross-gender sex from the service of reproduction.

Cross-gender couplings began to enjoy greater reproductive control and freer sexual involvement. The condom also proved effective at inhibiting the transmission of many opportunistic venereal diseases. The later development of the female birth-control pill further liberated sexual engagements between women and men.

Neither the condom nor the pill, however, has proved a hundred percent effective in the liberation of sex or the achievement of conscious reproductive control. Either may fail resulting in unwanted pregnancies. Only sexual abstinence and permanent, reproductive sterilization completely eliminate the risk of undesired pregnancy resulting from cross-gender sexual involvement. Sexual abstinence excludes all the benefits of sex along with the risk of sexually transmitted disease.

Although certain herbal concoctions were available for both men and women (before our age of modern medicine), the most common method of permanent, reproductive sterilization was castration (the removal of a man's testicles and sometimes penis).

Understandably, very few volunteered for this procedure. It was usually imposed as a punishment, or as a means of controlling the slave population. (The Catholic Church once employed castration to preserve the youthful pitch of certain male vocalists.)

Castration generally put an end to a man's sexual interest as well as his ability to breed. Our modern age of medicine, thankfully, provides us with methods of surgical sterilization which are far less drastic, available to both genders and which permit normal sexual function and appetite.

These procedures are well suited to those who choose permanent sterilization.

Sterilization is a responsible choice for those who suffer from serious genetic deformities or disease. Their parental aspirations should find more productive fulfillment though the adoption of the genetically sound progeny of others. Those who choose to remain reproductively viable must rely on other agencies for sexual fulfillment and reproductive control.

The most universally available avenue for sexual fulfillment and gratification is also the safest and least complicated. It is every bit as free from the risk of unwanted pregnancy as reproductive sterilization, and is equal to celibacy for avoiding the risk of venereal diseases.

Masturbation, as the sexual opportunity most readily available to everyone, can deliver practically every benefit sex has to offer. (Even infants are disposed to engage in this activity until they are repeatedly discouraged from it.) It is also, unfortunately, the most underrated sexual practice of all.

The practice of autonomous sexuality is common to most mammalian species as the primary means of relieving frustrated reproductive drives, or of discharging excessive accumulations of semen. This practice is most frequently indulged among primate species (especially monkeys, chimpanzees and man).

Animal masturbation should not be

confused with genital grooming (cleaning), nor can it properly be viewed as sexual in the human sense of the word (such comparisons are inaccurate and demeaning of our human activity). Erotic masturbation is a uniquely human practice in the service of our existential celebration.

Our practice of masturbation is sexual in the sense that it provides a sensual means for our emotional celebration of life and an intensely intimate expression of self-love and esteem. Its unique benefit, however, is that it does so apart from the appraisal, permission or approval of others[30]. Masturbation is self-

---

[30]   Masturbation can also be used to negate your spouse and/or partner's attempts to control you by withholding sex.

serve. As such, the quality of the experience it provides is a reflection of self-appraisal. At its best, auto-sexual masturbation is a self-reliant declaration of self-worth and sufficiency.

Despite its many benefits and near-zero risk factor, solo-sexual gratification (masturbation[31]) has never received the recognition and praise it so thoroughly deserves. This is partly due to a rather negative attitude commonly held towards masturbation.

Many mistakenly view the practice of

---

[31]   I herein declare January 13th (my birthday) World Masturbation Day, and to encourage everyone to make a special effort to pleasure themselves on this particular day. Of course this doesn't mean people shouldn't masturbate all year long as well.

auto-sexual gratification as an admission of defeat in the pursuit of interpersonal relations. Such individuals are unable to fully enjoy or achieve the benefits of sexual self-involvement.

Because they view it only as a means to quickly alleviate their frustration, they fail to approach masturbation as a sexual experience. They focus all their attention and effort on their primary reproductive center (ignoring the rest of their body) to obtain the most rapid sexual release.

The results of this approach are generally tinged with a deep sense of disappointment, an aftertaste of despair. A more positive attitude produces more rewarding effects and bestows a special advantage.

All those who view masturbation as an autonomous approach to self-gratification, revel in the full bounty of the experience it provides. They stimulate and employ the sensations of their entire body and being in their solitary approach to sexual ecstasy and orgasmic release.

Mind, nipples, skin and anus join genitalia as centers of sexual excitement and arousal. (A variety of sexual aids may also be employed.) Not until the moment of climax do the genitals command the sum of their attention.

Climax explodes with the euphoria of existential rapture and lingers in an aftermath of profound contentment. This, at least, is the soul-enriching experience of those who embrace masturbation as a self-sufficient means to sexual attainment.

The special advantage masturbation grants to the mindful practitioner, is a position of strength in the pursuit of romantic relations. Being sexually sufficient within one's self, allows for a more relaxed and confident approach, as opposed to the desperate questing of those who are incomplete.

Unfortunately, the frustration and despair of the forlorn are not the only obstacles to the guiltless abandon of auto-sexual delight. As with all things sexual, masturbation continues to suffer the slanderous attacks of the sex-hating, indolent elite and their joy-squelching, prudish adherents.

The despoilers of human pleasure are the forces behind such ridiculous absurdities as the notion that frequent masturbation causes blindness, insanity or hairy palms. (One dictionary, reflecting such influences, identifies self-abuse as a synonym of masturbation, falsely implying that the practice is somehow harmful.)

As idiotic as these notions are, they are only mild aspersions compared to the pleasure damner's favorite attack on masturbation. This attack consists of the willful misidentification of masturbation as Onanism. Onanism refers to the Biblical sin of Onan when he dishonestly shirked his duty towards his deceased brother.

The brief account of Onan (Genesis 38, 4-10) centers around a matter of Judaic tradition, custom and law, at a time when these terms were synonymous with each other. If a man died without offspring, after taking a wife, it fell upon his surviving brother to mate with his widow and sire an heir to continue his name. This is the situation which confronted Onan. His brother Er, had died leaving no progeny. It fell upon Onan to sire offspring on his brothers behalf.

Onan, however, had no such intention. He had the right to refuse, but doing so would have resulted in his disgrace (Deuteronomy 25, 5-10). Furthermore, Onan may have desired the opportunity for sexual congress which this custom provided. Onan chose to accept this opportunity, but withheld his seed by spilling it on the ground.

This was the sin of Onan, not any act of auto-sexual gratification. It was because of his dishonest abuse of custom that Onan was slain by his "God," according to Judaic myth.

Were masturbation the real issue of this account, then it was most unfair for "God" to kill Onan when thousands before him indulged in the same practice and got off scott-free. Onan was far from history's first masturbator.

Once a month, every fertile woman produces one mature ovum, however, each time a man ejaculates he releases about two million sperm, only one of which will fertilize an   egg[32].   The   other   one   million,   nine

---

[32]   The enormous disparity between the number of sperm issued by land dwelling animals (including man) and the number of eggs to be fertilized, can be traced all the way back to our most distant, ocean-dwelling ancestors, who spawned beneath the waves in the same manner as modern fish and amphibians. For such animals, the reproductive strategy consists of the female laying a cluster of unfertilized ovum on the ocean floor. The male then swims across the clutch spreading his milt over as many eggs as possible. Under this program, there is a much closer ratio of eggs to sperm than in present day land animals and aquatic mammals. Such eggs become fertilized and develop outside the female's body, just as sperm dose with respect to the male. This allowed the female to produce a great many more offspring than animals whose eggs are fertilized and/or gestated internally. As evolution carried forward into fish whose eggs were fertilized internally and later into mammals, where fertilization and gestation both occur within the female, evolutionary pressures forced a decrease in the number of eggs produced at one time. For the male, however, there were few, if any, pressures to reduce the number of sperm released, as insemination and

hundred, ninety nine thousand, nine hundred and ninety-nine are completely wasted, so it is extremely unlikely that "God" would be

---

gestation continued to occur outside the male's body, and the production of semen continued to be quite inexpensive. This is the cause for the overwhelming difference between the number of eggs produced vs. the number of sperm deployed to fertilize them. On the other hand, if a "supreme being" had engineered all life on earth, "It" would most likely have designed the male reproductive system to release only enough sperm to fertilize the females' eggs and little else.

concerned over some spilled semen.

Since only one sperm will join with an ovum, this is the only sperm which is actually wasted by masturbation. The rest would be wasted by "God's" design anyway (if such a being actually existed).

In their efforts to dominate and control the productive, upon whom they depend, the parasites among us use the story of Onan to condemn masturbation as a sin against the imaginary "God" they have conditioned others to believe in. They accomplish this by preaching that "God" slew Onan for spilling his semen on the ground without any reference to the circumstances surrounding the story.

Through this means, these spiritual

tyrants equate auto-sexual gratification with such transgressions as fornication and adultery (both were punishable by death). The purpose behind this distortion is both to reinforce reproductive coupling as the only acceptable, sexual outlet and to infect autonomous fulfillment with esteem-corroding guilt.

Guilt, in turn, acts to undermine confidence generating self-doubt and a profound sense of inadequacy, the prerequisites for the unquestioned acceptance of unfounded assertions of arbitrary, external authority.

A vague reference to an "...uncleanness that chanceth him by night..." (Deuteronomy 23, 10), has been used as a disparagement of masturbation, semen, and sex in general. The verse is commonly believed to refer to a nocturnal emission (a wet dream) but, considering the surrounding context, it could just as easily refer to urination (bed wetting), or a bout of diarrhea.

Taking this uncleanness as an involuntary spilling of sperm, however, allowed religious authorities to promote the idea that semen made one spiritually impure. To intentionally risk such pollution through auto-sexual stimulation, therefore, had to be among the bases of sins.

In the Middle-Ages, nocturnal emissions took on an even more sinister interpretation. They were believed to be the result of demonic possessions by succubae (in the case of male victims) or incubi (in the case of women). This superstitious fear of wet dreams contributed to the vampire legends. (Interestingly, in Bram Stoker's "Dracula," the vampire is depicted as having hairy palms.)

BREAKING THE CHAINS

Fortunately, for the rest of us, the machinations of clergy and potentates are losing their influence and power. The misrepresentations and twisting of recorded myths, used to promote their agendas of control are collapsing. Their demise is due, in part, to the achievement of a man named Gutenberg and his defiant stand against the

Catholic church. When Johann Gutenberg invented movable type in the fourteenth century, he opened the way to the mass production of books and broke the monopoly the Catholic church held over all learning.

Prior to Gutenberg, all books had to be copied by hand. The time and effort it took to reproduce a single copy was enormous. As a result, books were very expensive and owning one was well beyond the means of the average person. The Catholic church alone possessed the resources needed to provide publication. Only the nobility held sufficient wealth for purchase.

The average person could neither read nor write and was actively discouraged from learning. To the authorities of the time, the prospect of an educated populace posed a greater threat than famine or war.

Authorities of church and state depended on the ignorance of the masses and the manipulation of recorded myths, with the expository teachings of the Bible, to exercise control and demand the submission of their subjects. To secure their authority they had to maintain exclusive control over these writings.

For this reason, the average person was prohibited from owning or even reading the Bible. The authority of the clergy was beyond questioning. The text and meaning of the holy writings were whatever the religious authorities claimed. No one, apart from the church, could prove, or even know, otherwise.

The creation of movable type greatly reduced the cost of publication and the expense of book ownership. Gutenberg was willing to sell his publications to anyone who could pay his price. Books became both more affordable and available. The publishing monopoly of the church was broken.

Gutenberg defied the exclusive control the Catholic church held over scripture. He chose the Bible as the first large work to be published with his movable type. The Gutenberg Bible became the first collection of Judaic-Christian scripture available to individuals outside the clergy and ruling class.

As the Bible became accessible to anyone who could read, the misrepresentations of the clergy were exposed. The mindful reader could examine the story of Onan, understand its context and perceive it bore no connection to auto-sexual-gratification. Many other distortions were also revealed.

The few who could read began to teach those who wished to learn. Individuals acquired the knowledge and courage to dispute the teaching of the church. New religious sects formed around rival interpretations of scripture. A religious reformation had begun.

At first, this reformation had little affect regarding sexual matters. The Bible does, in fact, contain a harsh reproductive/sexual code, prescribing death for a wide range of infractions (Leviticus 20, 10-21). This allowed the clergy to maintain its repressive control over sex, despite the collapse of their scriptural distortions. The new clergies followed the old in condemning sexual pleasure and restricting it to its reproductive role within monogamous marriage.

Jesus had propagated the idea of a thought crime/sin when he declared a man guilty of adultery if he even looked at a woman with a lustful eye (Matthew 5, 28). This condemnation was applied, by extension, to masturbation which frequently involves imaginary, sexual imagery. (Although it is possible, with practice and effort, to masturbate without it.) If this notion were actually applied in practice, it could subject everyone who purchased or viewed pornographic material to execution for adultery or fornication.

The opportunity to read scripture oneself, however, did more than reveal the machinations of the clergy. It allowed the mindful reader to confront the many inconsistencies, contradictions, bigotries, errors and absurdities within the Bible itself.

In time, the more courageous began to question not only the authority of the church, but also that of the scripture and even the existence of a "God." Everything became subject to re-examination through the application of reason to experience and observation. Sexual attitudes became subject to change.

Over five hundred years have passed since the invention of movable type, the Gutenberg Bible and the beginning of the religious reformation. The sexual tyranny of the pretentious, power-seeking elite, however, continues to afflict us.

Within this decade (the 1990s) the Surgeon General of an allegedly free country (the United States of America) was removed from her office for broaching the subject of masturbation before an audience of Catholic, Islamic and Judaic clergy, regarding the problem of over population. The name of this outspoken, progressive woman was Joycelyn Elders.

Despite this and other setbacks, the revolution continues and succeeds. Reason and knowledge persist in dispelling the darkness of ignorance, superstition and oppression.

Psychologists and medical experts agree that auto-sexual gratification is both wholesome and normal. Masturbation provides monogamous couples with a means to compensate for differences in sexual appetite.

It also serves as a responsible outlet for individuals afflicted with serious genetic deformities or disease, those who suffer from incurable sexual infections and those whose sexual inclinations might place their lives and liberty at risk within an intolerant society. Masturbation is not, however, always synonymous with auto-sexual gratification.

Reciprocal masturbation and mutual fondling can play an important role in sexual foreplay for couples. They also provide couples and groups with the opportunity to share and explore sexual pleasures and practices apart from reproductive intercourse and the risk of pregnancy.

A WORLD OF INDULGENCE

Another opportunity for sexual fulfillment and existential celebration is also as free from the risk of unintended pregnancy as sexual abstinence, reproductive sterilization and auto-sexual gratification.

Unlike sexual abstinence and auto-sexual delight, however, it provides an avenue for the most intimate expression of friendship, admiration, affection and love. This dimension of sexual attainment is the practice of monogender, or unigender, sexual congress.

When individuals of the same gender engage in sexual relations, the possibility of producing offspring is nonexistent. This, however, is far from the only benefit to be derived from such relations. Single-gender sex provides an opportunity for the sensual appreciation and empathetic understanding of one's own gender which is unavailable through any other means. No male can understand or accurately empathize with the gender specific, emotional experiences or sensations of a woman.

He can, however, fully identify with the gender specific sensations of another man. Moreover, the same is true of women in regard to their relations with others. For this reason monogender sex represents the ultimate consummation of same gender bonding[33].

---

[33]   Many heterosexuals are so hetero-centric that they simply must impose their own sexual dynamics onto everyone else. So, because a heterosexual couple is made up of a man and a woman, every other form of sexuality must conform to the hetero pattern in some respect. Therefore, heterosexuals often insist that homosexual couples must contain a man and a female-substitute-male, or a women and a male-substitute-female. The idea that two men can enjoy each other sexually, as men, or that two women can enjoy one another, as women, is so foreign to many heterosexuals as to be beyond their conception. Unfortunately, many homosexuals buy-in to this nonsense and adopt this stereotype, which comes not from homosexuality, but from a repro-

Single-gender, unigender and mono-gender sex are all just creative ways of saying homosexual, but that's what we're talking about. If the world were mostly gay, what might the benefits be?

Well, for one, the rate of population growth would slow quite a bit. Also the value and care of children would increase and improve. Since homosexuals cannot reproduce with their partners, they must go outside of their relationships to find a member(s) of the opposite sex to have (a) child(ren) in the traditional way, or opt for

ductive imperative.

artificial insemination.

Under such a social structure those seeking children would be much more likely to have some actual money to care for (a) child(ren). It is also likely that more people would adopt in such a situation.

Homosexuality could actually improve the human species by encouraging people to choose their reproductive mates on the basis of beauty, intelligence, and health; instead of love. Furthermore, within such a society, people would be continually free to shop for the best genetic material for each child they chose to bring into the world. Moreover, the practice of gay sex is open to everyone, despite some opinions to the contrary.

Because same-gender-sex never produces offspring, the taboos regulating reproductive sex are pointless and without meaning, inside a homosexual context, and can be safely ignored. Therefore, if a father has mutually consenting sex with his grown son there's no harm done and no reason for either to be ashamed[34].

The same is true of homosexual relations between freely consenting brothers, same-gender-cousins[35], uncles and their adult nephews, even grandfathers and their grown grandsons. As long as everyone feels com-

---

[34]   Unless either of them is breaking his vows to another, such as to a wife or husband, of promised fidelity.

[35]   This section is about adult to adult relations only, including freely consenting brothers and same-gender-cousins.

fortable and unforced in such sexual relations, there's no reason to feel ashamed in them. The same reality exists with regard to sexual relations between women toward each other.

Several surveys and studies show, when either of two identical twins is gay, fifty-one percent of the time, the other twin is gay too. This information is commonly used to show homosexuality is genetic. If this were true, however, a percentage much closer to a hundred should be expected.

The "it's genetic" crowd is just trying to avoid responsibility for the way they are, but no excuse is needed. Homosexuality is a legitimate choice anyone can make, one offering many benefits to societies and individuals alike. So, come join the party, if you will.

LOVER WANTED

My ideal man is no older than thirty and no younger than eighteen. He has straight, black hair and medium brown skin. He is no taller than six foot and is of aboriginal-American, Asian, or Mexican decent. My ideal guy is intelligent without being condescending. He is trim and lean. Ideally, he should be uncut with a smooth body and a boyish face. At best, he should be versatile, sexually, but I can wait a little for him to become so. This is my ideal, but I may consider others depending on how close they are to what I have described here. As for myself, I am white and a little overweight, but I am working on that. I have my own home and a great car, for anyone who cares about such things. Interested parties may email me at:

RayGreaves2@yahoo.com